HOW
TO BE
OLD

HOW TO BE OLD

LESSONS IN LIVING BOLDLY FROM THE
ACCIDENTAL ICON

LYN SLATER

PLUME

PLUME

An imprint of Penguin Random House LLC
penguinrandomhouse.com

LIBRARY OF CONGRESS CATALOGING-IN-PUBLICATION DATA

Names: Slater, Lyn, author.
Title: How to be old: lessons in living boldly from
the accidental icon / Lyn Slater.
Description: New York: Plume, Penguin Random House, [2024]
Identifiers: LCCN 2023038164 (print) | LCCN 2023038165 (ebook) |
ISBN 9780593471791 (hardcover) | ISBN 9780593471814 (ebook)
Subjects: LCSH: Self-acceptance. | Older people—Biography.
Classification: LCC BF575.S37 S62 2024 (print) |
LCC BF575.S37 (ebook) | DDC 158.1—dc23/eng/20231218
LC record available at https://lccn.loc.gov/2023038164
LC ebook record available at https://lccn.loc.gov/2023038165

Printed in the United States of America

1st Printing

BOOK DESIGN BY SHANNON NICOLE PLUNKETT

This book is dedicated to my mother,
who taught me how much fun it is
to be a belligerent woman.

CONTENTS

Prologue

The year I turned fifty-nine, I couldn't find any-thing to wear. Everything that hung in my closet or on racks in stores no longer inspired. This out-of-sorts feeling tells me I am ready for a new story to tell. Something new to get dressed in. Clothes have always helped me tell stories about myself; who I am, who I wish to be. They could be chapters of a memoir.

I look toward the end of a decade with excitement, eager to take stock of what I've achieved, and to the new decade ahead for possibility. When I look back on each phase of my life, I remember the experiences I had, not what age I was when I had them. I don't view each birthday as a lost year of youth, but as a new stage of opportunity. Instead of thinking about all the things I'll miss about the past, I focus on the things I can do in the moment that make my life exciting. For me, that means styling a new look, taking on new roles, having new experiences. Perhaps finding a new place to live or a new way of working. I go back to school to learn some-thing new.

During my fifties, I completed a PhD and became a full-time professor. My daughter graduated from college, found her profession, and married. I took my first trip to Europe. I had a hip replacement. I learned how to make jewelry and started to take classes in a fashion school. I lived in a loft in Williamsburg. My father died; my sister had three babies. My partner Calvin and I grew as a couple and learned the right way to have a fight. We moved from Brooklyn to Queens. I stopped dyeing my hair and cut it short.

After the hip replacement, I could move freely without pain for the first time in two years. I paid for graduate school for me, college and a wedding for my daughter. I saved $250 a month by no longer dyeing my fast-growing hair. This gave me a few more resources to invest in whatever new "wardrobe" I wanted to design. During this decade, from each of my experiences, I learned important life lessons and gained new skills. Taking classes in a fashion school and traveling to Europe for the first time in my life triggered an unrealized desire I did not know I had. It was still undefined, and yet I felt its urgency. It was a hand on my back, pushing me out the door.

But first, I had to find something to wear.

Many people, no matter what age they are, search for meaning as a new decade approaches. So many people kept asking me how I felt about turning sixty when at fifty-nine my age was the last thing on my mind. I quickly discovered that the sixties is a tough decade. Truly, I did not think of myself as old until everyone started telling me I was. These are the things no one prepared me for. AARP relentlessly sends you membership applications. You receive frequent reminders that you must sign up for Medicare three months before your sixty-fifth birthday, or else you'll get a fine. You can collect Social Security. People ask when you plan to "retire." You are eligible for senior discounts on trains, at movie theaters, museums. They ask if you want to take advantage of these, or it's assumed that you do because of the color of your hair. Parents begin to pass away if they haven't already. People jump up to give you a seat on the subway. You are told you look good . . . for your age. Cemeteries send you flyers in the mail, telling you it's time to buy a plot. During a pandemic, you are told you are in the group most likely to die.

Why would I allow my age, only just a number after all, to define who I am or determine how I live my life? Why does everyone feel compelled to keep reminding me of it? Especially because I, like everyone else, am so much more than my age. I, like everyone else, am aging uniquely, so I don't understand why suddenly the edges of my individuality are being sanded down so I can be lumped in with everyone else. How old I am is hands down the most boring fact about me. I became determined at fifty-nine not to let age define me, or get in my way. It was not clear to me yet what I would do, but I was certain that because of my inherently rebellious nature I would find a way, as I always have, to challenge expectations set by others. Expectations that try to dictate who I could be or what I could do. All the reminders that I was getting old only served to provoke me. They fueled my desire to make this decade one where I will resist stereotypes that dictate what I should look like or how I should live life when I am old. I will use my creativity to write an alternative story, a story born of gleeful defiance of the idea that it is time for me to gracefully bow out and disappear.

So here I am again, now sixty-nine, soon to be seventy. Another decade has passed. I've moved from the city, bought a house with my partner; a deepening of our commitment to each other and our family. I became a grandmother at the beginning of the decade and again at the end. I decided what kind of grandmother I wanted to be. I came to accept my identity as a writer. I retired from teaching after twenty years. I continue to work as a social work consultant. I had cataract surgery and can see better than I have in years. I had Covid, yet gratefully continue to survive the pandemic. My mother died. My sister's babies are in college. I've been to Shanghai, Tokyo, Madrid, Paris, Lisbon, Reykjavik, Amsterdam, Cologne, Basel, and London—some of those cities more than once. International fashion campaigns have featured me, as has the fashion press. I have more than half a million followers on Instagram. There are commercials, music videos, *Today Show* appearances, and . . . well, let's not go there yet.

During this past decade of my life, I've had the most incredible adventure. It's so far outside my expectations for what my sixties would bring that even I don't fully understand how it all happened. During this last decade, a professor of social work, a grandmother with gray hair and wrinkles, became a fashion star. Somehow an ordinary woman like me found herself living an extraordinary older life as my alter ego, known as Accidental Icon. Ironically, during the years when society assumed I would become invisible as an older woman, I was more visible than at any other time of my life. Infinitely more visible than when I was young.

As I review each year and reflect on my experiences, I hope to learn the whys and hows of what I did or didn't do to make this adventure happen. I invite you to come along with me. I discover important lessons about how to be old. I learn the importance of remaining true to yourself and your values. I learn how powerful stereotypes about age are. I learn that if you are not attentive, they can derail you despite how badass you think you are. I learn how to not let my age define me even when others want it to. I understand it's a choice each day to not let being older get in the way of living the life I want to live.

Ending one decade and beginning another, no matter how old we are, implies the question "What now?" Societal and familial expectations and our own unique circumstances complicate our response to this question. I am aware that, as a white, educated, cis, healthy woman with financial security, my privilege has contributed to what I could do at sixty and how I could do it. It informs what I can do now. Growing older is also a privilege, one not enjoyed by all. Yet before it happens to us, we see being old as something to avoid at all costs. The dictionary definition of the word *old* is "having lived a long time." I ask in all sincerity: Would you really prefer the alternative to living a long time? As I turn seventy this year, I will gratefully add "old" to my list of privileges and recognize it as such.

There is one aspect of getting older that is under our control: how we choose to think about our age. What we think about getting or being old informs the way we feel about ourselves as people who are and will age. It impacts our health. It influences how we might respond to the challenges and opportunities older life poses. Nothing about your age, regardless of whether you are turning thirty or one hundred, should deter you from living the life you want to, regardless of what others say or society says you should or can do. I write this book as I look toward seventy. Just as I did when I was fifty-nine, I review each year of the past decade. During my sixties, I lived a life online as the Accidental Icon. I'll share the highs and lows, the joys and sorrows, the gains and losses, of my time being her. But most importantly, as I revisit each year, I offer a lesson learned, lessons that can help you respond creatively, no matter what age you are, to the challenges and opportunities that life may send your way. These are lessons that I take with me as I begin my next decade, another opportunity for adventure. I know it will be an adventure because, like before, I am determined to make it one. My body and the world have changed, and once again I'm finding my clothes no longer fit. It's time to write a new story, to reuse in imaginative ways garments that already hang in my closet. I remain engaged in the extraordinary process of aging, a process—as fashion icon extraordinaire

David Bowie once said—"whereby you become the person you always should have been." Becoming is a process in motion and implies hope. I will become that person. What's most exciting is, I don't quite yet know who she will be.

I can't wait to see what experiences I'll be looking back on when I'm about to turn eighty, and what possibilities might lie ahead. After all, my mother lived until ninety-five. But for now, I'm going to turn back and see what I can bring with me as I turn seventy. I'll remember what I have learned about how to be old; I'll find pearls of wisdom and gemstones of insight that reflect the light, embellishments that add beauty and sparkle to whatever I may decide to wear. That makes me, an older woman, someone of value in the world.

60

Predict the Future
by Inventing It

Today is the first day of the fall 2013 semester. Anxiety taps me on the shoulder, waking me up, and excitement propels me out of bed as I slip into my role of teacher. As a professor of social work and law, I know that every class I teach brings new students and new perspectives. The students and I will leave as different people than the ones who entered the room. It's that potential that excites me. Still, I know I'll have to wait through the first few classes to understand who is in the room and where we might go together. I've learned to be patient, comfortable with not knowing, because that's part of the class's process of becoming. I am dressed in black from head to toe. I wear a suit designed by the Japanese fashion designer Yohji Yamamoto. I found it in a consignment store in Brooklyn. So today, while first-day-of-school anxiety beats its wings in my stomach, my black-and-white oxfords fly toward the subway that will take me downtown. My layered white hair blows in the wind. My statement earrings chime with each step, announcing I am on the way.

Before the first day of classes, I search the internet for an activity that will introduce the students and me to each other in a way that is not boring and repetitive. What I decide to wear is how I will make myself known. In the professional school where I teach, the dress code is formal: suits, tailored trousers, skirts, and blouses. Social work has always preoccupied itself with status. Like other care-oriented careers, fields historically considered to be women's work, social work emerged as a way for middle-class women to get out of the house and into the world. It has never achieved the status or the pay reserved for male-dominated careers. Our professional garb self-consciously mimics that of professors in the school of law and the business school. I may not wear jeans, not even on Friday, when we sit in meandering committee meetings I am mandated to attend as part of my service requirement. I must devote a certain amount of my time to be used for the benefit of my school, independent of my own scholarship. These days, service feels more like penance than something I will be rewarded for. We argue over master syllabi I must use but rarely agree with because they teach students about what is, rather than engage them to think about what could be. This approach to learning makes me feel constrained, restless, and bored. My Catholic education compels me to confess that I close my classroom door, ignore the syllabus, and do what I want. While that's a partial solution to the dilemma I face as an academic in an increasingly corporatized institution, it does not offer the challenge I feel I must have to grow.

It was during the late 1990s that I was introduced to the designs of Yohji Yamamoto. What first intrigued me was how he pushed the boundaries on suits. He works in black with touches of white, calling forth a somber seriousness. I fell in love with Yohji when I first read what he said about black: "Black is modest and arrogant at the same time. Black is lazy and easy—but mysterious. But above all black says this: 'I don't bother you—don't bother me.'" His designs blur the distinction between womenswear and menswear, using theatrical drapes that create space between the body and the garment, erasing symmetry and proportion.

I think what Yamamoto knows about everyone is that as humans we are never perfect. In fact, we are quite flawed, and when we are aware of this, we feel vulnerable. When I put on Yamamoto's garments—irregular, with ripped and ragged fabrics and hems—perfection becomes mundane. I have permission to be messy, defiant, imperfect, and unfinished. At the same time I feel feminine, beautiful, and sensual in the space between my body and the drape of the clothes. The word *trickster* comes to mind when I think of Yohji.

The draping of the garments Yohji creates triggers memories of the nuns who taught me from kindergarten through college, and of the Jesuits who populate the university where I now teach. In these spaces, there are many rules about what a woman can or cannot do with her body and what rooms she can enter. Black is the color not only of religious attire but also of judges' robes and academic gowns. When I wear this color, it suggests to my students that what we do here in the classroom is of great importance, as are they. When I present at a conference, I make sure that my outfit demands that I receive attention, so that my words might receive attention too. While my clothes from Yohji Yamamoto make me look utterly singular in the academic room, no one can make the claim that I am dressed "inappropriately" for the occasion. Standing on this edge, sometimes in danger of falling off, fills me with glee. The right outfit can really make a statement.

Today is the first day of the fall 2013 semester. As the subway rumbles downtown and I head toward the first day of class, this time I am not a professor in a social work school. My photo ID shows that today I am a continuing education student in a fashion school. The class Building a Vintage Business begins at 6:20 p.m., and is in room SR7. It is twilight. I have taken classes at this fashion school before, most recently Jewelry Fabrication and Tailoring. Since entering this space, I have come into contact with fashion in a different way than what they show in glossy magazines under the control of editors. I become more and more excited by the potential of finding a way to do something involving fashion. I am anxious because I can't imagine how I might be part of that world. On this day, there is something about the subway ride that makes me feel like it's Cinderella's coach and I am headed to a ball I have not received an invitation to.

New York City is one of the fashion capitals of the world, and when I moved here, the epicenter was Manhattan. Unobtrusively, Brooklyn was encroaching on the territory. My partner Calvin and I recently moved to Manhattan, something that we could check off the bucket list. We both work in Manhattan. There is a garment district there. We found a small but light-filled modern condo on the Upper East Side, right where it turns into East Harlem. Our new neighborhood was developing or, to be transparent, gentrifying. What it would be was as of yet undetermined. Best of all, this apartment provided easy access to the campus where I teach, just a block away from Lincoln Center, a stylish gateway between Broadway and the Upper West Side that until 2015 was the home of New York Fashion Week.

When wandering the streets of Manhattan, one can always find style inspiration. As Bill Cunningham, the well-known *New York Times* street photographer, asserted, "The best fashion show is on the street. Always has been, and always will be." Living here, I admit to being influenced by the overabundance of black clothes that Manhattan artists and other intellectuals seem to favor. Black flatters any figure, and looks lovely with my hair, which is turning white. But I am also inspired by the vision of young people in Brooklyn who are styling thrift and vintage clothing in interesting ways and dyeing their hair gray. It seems this is a playful experimentation with the notion of "old." These same young people stop me on the street to ask if I work in "fashion."

In fashion-school classes I had taken previously, I had innovative ideas but often fell short on execution. I realized that it would take time, money, and practice to become a skilled fashion or jewelry designer and craftsperson. I felt as if there were someone breathing down my neck to do something different, and to make it happen now. In hindsight, I don't think I was looking to start something completely new; rather, I wanted to make something new with what I already had. As I look back at this time, I think the hot breath I felt was coming from my age. Although I couldn't yet name this anxiety, it was dawning on me that I did not have all the time in the world. If I wanted to do something adventurous in my life, the time was now.

———————————

There is a kind of aching sweetness to the outfit I choose for the first day of this fashion-school class, a counterbalance to the black edge I wore for the first day as a professor. I feel rather angelic. The long dress is white cotton, illuminating the encroaching darkness that comes with twilight. There is a hood I can wear if I need protection. The black in my oxfords is a wink to the coming night. The color white can reflect all the visible light of the spectrum and thus offers unlimited possibilities. It symbolizes new beginnings, wholeness, and completion. You cannot hide behind white because it easily becomes translucent. It offers a sense of calmness and protection. White is a blank page.

In spring 2013, not long before my sixtieth birthday in June, Yohji sent a woman with white hair like mine down the runway in an off-the-shoulder white cotton dress with a long, billowing skirt. The image was unexpected; I was not used to seeing an older woman in runway shows or in top fashion magazines. Titled *Cutting Age*, Yohji's show was a play on the idea of a garment's shelf life, the passing of seasons and, with them, of trends. Set in an architecturally important church in Berlin, it consisted of iconic pieces from the last thirty years of the designer's career, and told the story not only through the clothes but through the presence of older as well as young women models. Digging into the show's backstory, I discovered that the women were "real people," cast from the street the day before in an open call. I took a screenshot of the image, printed it out, and pasted it into my journal.

Now I enter the classroom, spread my long, flowing white skirt, and take my seat. In the classroom at the professional school where I teach, desks are arranged in rows that face a podium at the front of the room. In fashion school, there are long tables arranged in a square. We can spread out our notebooks, scatter our pens, empty our tote bags, and face each other. I open my journal, ready to take notes. Like the woman in Yohji's Berlin show, I am the oldest person in the room. Nobody here seems to care. They are way more interested in what I decide to wear.

The professor of the class, Bridgett Artise, is the author of a book called *Born Again Vintage: 25 Ways to Deconstruct, Reinvent, and Recycle Your Wardrobe.* An early pioneer in sustainable fashion, she sports a short Afro and favors very large retro-style glasses, turbans, head wraps, newsboy caps, and the designer Emilio Pucci. Her smile and her passion for what she sells in her store are infectious. In her case it is upcycled vintage clothes. Upcycled clothing takes an existing garment and improves it, whether by combining it with other garments and materials or adding ornamental flair, like using embroidery and patchwork to mend holes. Her opening line for class that first day: "There are several routes to a destination."

We start the class with a quick tour of fashion history, focused on the popular silhouettes. While the class covers the commercial aspects of what anyone would need to know to build a vintage business, what kind of vintage clothes each person decides to sell is a choice among unlimited possibilities. You can specialize in particular designers, focus your collecting on a particular era, or even sell just one product, like T-shirts or denim. We learn about the pros and cons of where to sell: brick-and-mortar or online. We study the merits of Etsy versus eBay. We are called upon to share our visions about what we would sell and how we might sell it. I am obsessed with the idea of upcycling vintage clothes. You don't have to be a perfect sewer to do this. The professor asks what we have done before that can inform our new venture. She encourages us to elaborate on our personalities, to transform them into a persona with a story. "This is a personality-driven business," she says.

As class progresses session by session and I appear in all my different Yohji-inspired outfits, the students who sit with me around the square in the room and those I pass in the hall tap my shoulder and say, "Wow, I really love your style." My professor tells me I have an as-yet-unidentified "talent" and an "eye." Two of my classmates find their way to seats on either side of me. They already have popular blogs about vintage fashion; a store will be their next evolution. One night one of them turns to me and says, "You should start a blog."

"You really think so?" I ask. I'm intrigued. That somehow feels more immediate and doable than starting a business. I could do a blog about upcycling. From that moment on, in between the notes I take about the care of vintage clothing and determining how to evaluate and name the condition of the clothes, I doodle and daydream a blog. I even have a working title: *Wardrobe Surgery*.

In order to upcycle, you need to seam rip. Seam ripping is when you take apart a piece of clothing, undoing all the seams that hold it together. Seam ripping can show you how to assemble clothes and how they are constructed. The second function of seam ripping is that it can "undo" mistakes and help you correct them. When you are working with vintage, upcycling inspires you to come up with a way to put whatever you're working on back together so that it becomes something modern and new. Our professor is an expert seam ripper and upcycler.

Adapting this lesson from sewing, I decide to lay out my past experiences like different pattern pieces of cloth that eventually become a garment. Scattered all over the table, they wait ready for me to see which can construct this project of starting a blog. Once I have inventoried the materials I have at my disposal, I will know what new notions I might need to pick up to make this come together.

The important pieces stand out like swatches of embellished textiles in a fabric store. We have decided that while I am a "vintage piece," I can put outfits together in a modern and cool way. Technology has fascinated me since 1975, when I punched cards for a computer the size of my Upper East Side living room. In 1991 I was the owner of the first clunky gray Apple laptop. I snagged a first-generation Blackberry. While other professors banned the laptops that appeared in classrooms in the mid-1990s, I allowed them in mine. I learned how to use web design platforms. In 2007 I designed a Ning site for my students in a club called the Social Work and Art Collective. I found and posted interesting content on it, and it grew to be the largest club in the school.

My area of research and expertise is interdisciplinary education, which means I know how to collaborate and talk with people in a field other than my own. I know how to find our commonalities. I love being around young people— probably because I am the oldest of six siblings—and as a professor I teach young people every day. I've worked with adolescents and young women for most of my career. I've conducted thousands of interviews. I've taken improv classes and can pivot on a dime. I can research and write, my two favorite pastimes. Because of my training and skill as a social worker and professor, I know how to engage people who are ready for a change or to learn something new, and those who are not. Oh, and might I mention that my partner Calvin is a physics lab inhabitant by day, ponytailed street photographer by night?

I already have what it takes to start a blog, I realize. Suddenly I am less anxious, and the beating wings in my stomach quiet down.

———————————

At the time, I thought little about why, out of all the courses in the fashion-school catalog, I took one about building a vintage business. Now I laugh at the irony that a professor who wrote the book about how to "deconstruct, reinvent, and recycle" taught the class. What is now clear is that by taking that class, I put myself into a space with a professor and classmates who treasured oldness manifested as vintage clothes. Regardless of our ages, we were excited about collecting these garments, repairing them, selling them, and transforming them into something new. We were using vintage pieces to be creative and express our diverse identities. Perhaps, subconsciously more aware and concerned about my age and aging than I believed myself to be, I wanted to know that I would still have value. That I still had the power for reinvention and self-invention. Why do we allow vintage clothes like denim jeans the freedom to age? Why does the worth of certain articles of clothing increase over time? Why do they become valued for their narrative stamina rather than fall out of favor, as older people seem to do?

Japanese designers attracted me because they were so committed to resisting norms of youth and beauty. They made clothes that showed wear and deterioration, but beautifully, in a way that celebrated imperfection and was, for me, a hopeful promise about being old. In one of my earliest posts, I am wearing a sweater by Junya Watanabe with holes, and a skirt that is frayed and ripped in a disorganized way. I see now, of course, why I wore them during this period of my life. They represented who I saw myself to be: an intellectual, a creative, and a woman aging.

I was searching for an understanding of how I would live my life as an older person, what possible identities I could assume, what potential existed in me despite the anxiety of not knowing about this new time of life.

And yet this was not the first nor the last occasion that I took time to consider what kind of life I wanted to live and identify who I might become. I expressed this quest during other times of my life through the clothes I wore and my propensity for constantly reinventing. Taking control of how you want to live your life and what story you want to tell about yourself is an act that transcends age. As each year passes during our lifetimes, through experiments and trial and error we are always figuring out how to respond to what life throws our way. If we change how we think, are willing to risk a little and experiment and view challenges as creative opportunities, suddenly anything is possible. Life when you are old could very well become an unpredictable, wild, and crazy adventure, as it has for me.

On my way to the last class of this semester in fashion school, I am stopped in the hall and asked if someone can take my photo as part of a new marketing campaign for the school. Another Yohji Yamamoto muse inspired my outfit on this day. The model wore a beautifully tailored black coat with a red tulle bustle. For this last class, I wear a long black skirt, a white blouse with long sleeves that cover my hands, and my familiar black-and-white oxfords. Red lipstick and a cropped angora wrap sweater are my red tulle bustle. For the first time in my life, a photographer other than someone in my family wants to take my photo. I could not have imagined that one day photographers would surround me, yelling at me to look their way, the clicking of their cameras like a cloud of locusts. But we're not at that part of the story yet.

I walked into that class thinking I would open a vintage store, and I walked out knowing I wanted to start a blog. I have so much gratitude for my professor and classmates for showing me that there is something to be said for looking back to see where you might next want to go. I learned to transform something old into something modern, something never seen before. What this blog would be about is another conversation. It's one thing to think about doing something; it's another to actually do it.

61

Take Advantage of Lucky Accidents

There are lots of versions on the internet of the story about how I became famous. The clickbait version is a Cinderella story. One day I go to meet a friend for lunch at Lincoln Center during Fashion Week. Before my friend arrives, photographers mistakenly think I am someone in fashion and take my photo. Finding me surrounded by a crowd, said friend declares, "You're an accidental icon!" and that is how I named my blog. According to articles about me, that is also the day I magically become famous, and my life was transformed.

Here's what really happened. It's true I met a friend at Lincoln Center, though we weren't there by accident. We were there for a Fashion Week event in early September 2014. The friend was a fashion editor I met in Montreal the month before. Photographers took my photo. Journalists from Japan, who had spotted my Yohji suit a mile away, interviewed me on the street. And while this moment was, in retrospect, a turning point, the fact is, my blog already had a name.

I put up my first Instagram and blog post on August 27, 2014. It took me three more years of posting to "get famous," or at least until I got a modeling contract that put me on the cultural radar screen and into airplanes that took me all over the world. In the meantime, my ordinary life continued. I taught classes, went to faculty meetings, babysat my granddaughter, cooked dinner, visited my mother, met friends for coffee, did the laundry, and cleaned my bathroom. I had hardly become an icon.

I am sitting on a step in front of a cast-iron building in SoHo with large windows. Behind them, under soaring ceilings, stand mannequins dressed in black. There is a banner that proclaims "IF SoHo, New York." It is early August. It is unbearably hot. Next to me are three young men dressed in black and white. Two of them wear different versions of a short jumpsuit. They are quite unlike the other young men dressed in jeans who pass by us on the sidewalk. I'm wearing a Yamamoto black jersey garment. It is not what it appears to be. It looks like a dress but is actually asymmetrical culottes. My sandals, I scored in a vintage store called Beacon's Closet, and they rest on a cross-hatched plate of iron, as does my leather bag. I have on large black cat's-eye sunglasses. My earrings are from Paris, black-and-white layered plastic suggesting an art deco ladybug. We are in line for a sale that only happens two times a year. I am near the front.

IF Boutique is probably the oldest store still open in SoHo. It has survived gentrification and the pandemic. In the 1970s, situating a boutique on the corner of Greene Street and Grand was a risk; developers had not yet gotten their hands on the area south of Houston, and it was still considered one of the grittiest and most dangerous parts of the city. The story is told that the audacity of the move appalled but impressed Andy Warhol, and he gave IF free advertising on the back page of *Interview* for a year.

The boutique garnered the reputation of being the first in New York to sell designers such as Yohji Yamamoto, Maison Martin Margiela, Ann Demeulemeester, Dries Van Noten, and Jean Paul Gaultier, designers that reflect my own style in a profound way. I am oppositional by nature. Status quo is my archenemy; boredom feels like death. So it stands to reason that I am obsessed with avant-garde designers. We are kindred spirits. These were the first designers who sent older women down the runway. When I wear their clothes, I feel they make a space for me. These sentiments are echoed in the choices I make on my blog, especially those I made in its early days.

The aesthetic of IF Boutique is described as "dressed-down luxury." The garments that hang on the long racks against the wall can be thrown on in a way that makes the wearer appear quite nonchalant. There are no concessions to what is in fashion today, or what was in style yesterday. I covet the clothes, shoes, and accessories that live in this store. At this time, to my chagrin, I cannot afford them. But as I have learned, there are several routes to a destination.

Twice a year, in February and August, IF has what is known as the Basement Sale, when you can find all the above designers for up to 85 percent off. Suddenly, thousand-dollar garments become affordable. Rumor has it that some people actually fly in from other cities for the sale. About an hour before the opening, men and women dressed almost exclusively in black and white slowly begin to form a long, curving line around the block. The line itself is a street-style fashion show of the bold, the avant-garde, and the adventurous. When the doors open, there is a beeline to the stairs, boots (everyone here is wearing them, even in this summer heat) clomping loudly on the wide-plank wood floors and down the iron steps.

The basement today feels like a crowded subway car with broken air conditioning. I approach the task at hand methodically, sifting through the items piece by piece, rack by rack, until I find what I am looking for and grab my seven permitted pieces. I press into the packed dressing room with a Y's embroidered pants and jacket, Ann Demeulemeester black pants with dangling ties and buckles at the ankle, and a Junya Watanabe sweater with holes. There is hardly room to change, and getting to the mirror is an impossible task. Despite this, I determine that the pieces in my hand, which I can only just afford, are worth fighting for, and so I push to the line to pay.

The closer I get, the narrower my vision and the harder it is to breathe. When I finally get to the front, I am about to faint. I ask the black-and-white-clad (I think it's last season's Marc Le Bihan) woman at the register if I can sit on the stool behind her and put my head down. In the blink of an eye, the store's gallant creative director, Phillip, is pushing a glass of cold water into my hand, and the lovely woman is coaching me to breathe. After a moment or two, I perk up. Then, perched on the high stool, legs crossed, I chat with the staff and customers until I reach a state of full recovery. At some point, rather frenzied shoppers approach me and ask if I work there. Concerned I might take offense, the woman who sits next to me, swiping cards, says, "You know that's an enormous compliment, right? Staff are known for our style." I take it as one, and as yet another sign I am on the right path.

While I was in line at the IF Basement Sale, Calvin snapped a photo of me in the company of other members of the avant-garde fashion scene. This is the photo I will choose for my first blog and Instagram post, a post I end with these words:

> *So, I am thinking if I got this far "accidentally," how far could I really go if I learn and think about fashion with people who really do it and know it? Since I always do my best thinking and learning in the company of others, to those of you "in the know," or who are "becoming" too, I invite you to come to think, talk and learn with me about fashion and take on the project of making my icon status (and yours) less accidental!*

Some years later, I can't remember exactly when, I will change my Instagram profile to read: "BTW no longer accidental."

People didn't start the very first personal style blogs as launchpads for fame or money, as they often do now. Many of these blogs began innocently as creative outlets, like mine was intended to be. The earliest bloggers, like Garance Doré, Tavi Gevinson, Susie Lau, and Leandra Medine, began their blogs as a hobby to indulge their love of fashion and writing. My blog was more like the early blogs than the ones populating the blogosphere by 2014. The road to fame and money was already paved through the amassing of followers, sponsored posts, and affiliate linking by that time, but I was still inhabiting a more personal space on the internet.

Until fashion blogging, fashion was a closed society of designers, editors, and retailers. They traditionally covered fashion in a hierarchical way through the legacy fashion magazines. The first generation of bloggers were contrarians. Perhaps that is why I identified with them more than any of the bloggers coming onto the scene when I was. The early blogs evidenced a keen awareness of technology and social media. Unlike magazines, they felt free in their expression. The first bloggers drew in hundreds of thousands of people like me, who enjoyed fashion but had been excluded from the conversation. Fashion editors hit back with articles that bloggers called "jealous, hypocritical and catty" and that reinforced the fashion world's reputation of being cold, ruthless, and unwelcoming. Those who love fashion can thank the first fashion bloggers for making fashion more democratic and forcing design houses, and ultimately fashion magazines, to accept a new reality. They opened the door, and I pushed my way through it.

I love Garance Doré for many reasons. I like her minimalist aesthetic and her French sensibility. She attracts not only women of her age but older women followers too. She is elegant and has a light touch. Her images are born from her days as a street photographer. They remain natural and unposed, with a subtle underlying sense of humor. Her writing is vulnerable, authentic, and real. She grows her hair and cuts it short over and over. She is a self-taught illustrator, photographer, HTML coder, and writer. She still wears clothes from Zara because when she started, they were all she could afford, but she makes them look expensive and stylish. She features interesting, creative women doing new and entrepreneurial things. Her video series (and, later, podcast) *Pardon My French* finds her interviewing fashion designers like Dries Van Noten and Kenzo. In 2015 she published a book titled *Love, Style, Life*, a kind of visual memoir featuring her illustrations and photographs.

Garance constantly reinvents herself, as she has done through her entire career. She moves cities, is in and out of relationships, changes the format of her blog. She has been a companion to me through the years, and I feel that while she was always a few steps ahead of me, ultimately we share parallel stories. I identify with her vulnerability, her honesty, and the uncertainty that quivers in her words from time to time. The idea that she can't really believe what has happened to her emanates from her writing at times, like a whiff of subtle perfume. There is a certain hesitation there, a shyness that I find in myself too. There is a question lingering in the rarefied air of fashion about really belonging.

In August 2014, the month before I launched my blog, I saw that Garance was going to be speaking at a Montreal Fashion Weekend event. Though we both lived in New York, I would happily follow her out of the country for a chance to meet. I pressed upon Calvin that we really needed to go. I had to meet her. I felt like there would be some magic karma, that something would rub off on me if I could see her in person. I can't explain my connection to her. We are the same, but very different.

We took an Amtrak to Montreal. Luckily, we found a fabulous little bed-and-breakfast, despite the crowd that had come to the city. We prepared ourselves to go to Garance's event, which was held in a bookstore and hosted by another fashion blogger named Lolita, well known in Montreal. The name of Lolita's blog was *Fashion Is Everywhere*. The following week she published the very first feature ever written about me. I dressed simply and elegantly in a white shirt and beautifully pleated wide-leg trousers by Kenzo. Before the talk, I recall having the best salad I ever ate in my life.

Garance was selling her original illustrations at the event. Having a tendency to imbue objects with magical properties, I wanted one as a talisman for good luck. I looked at them carefully, and one stood out. It was a pen-and-ink drawing of a small, girlish woman with a chin-length bob. She had the same nose as me. She wore a large pair of sunglasses. She carried an air of naiveté about her. A bare shoulder pointed forward, arching up as if to protect her vulnerability. A wisp of hair obscured her mouth. I made my purchase. I listened to the talk. I waited in line once again, this time to have Garance autograph the illustration.

The picture Calvin took is black and white. In it, Garance and I are sitting at a table, talking and looking at each other intensely. We are not smiling. I am telling her about Accidental Icon, my hopes and dreams for it. I ask her for advice. With a look that in retrospect I identify as a little sad, she tells me to never lose myself. That being authentic, doing it because you love it, is when you will be most attractive to people. It is when you will be happiest. She sighs, bends down, and writes, "For The Accidental Icon, Good Luck! Garance Doré."

Over the next few years, I would come to know the powerful truth behind her words.

I don't remember how I came up with the name Accidental Icon, but Calvin reminds me it had something to do with getting stopped on the street and being accidentally identified as someone who works in fashion. As I think about it now, it seems my intuition must have been working on overdrive. In truth it was the word *accidental* that somehow captured my imagination. I had a strong sense that this word just had to be in the name. When something is accidental, it happens by chance. It is both unintentional and unexpected. A lucky accident is something that is accidental but gives you a pleasant surprise. There could be no better description of how I felt about what would eventually happen to me over the next decade of my life. However, there was a more immediate reason that I, always the pragmatist, picked the name. When I put "Accidental Icon" into the domain search engine, to my surprise accidentalicon.com was available. A lucky accident. That sealed the deal.

———————————

We're at home today, August 14, 2014, in our Manhattan condo, with its white walls and black granite countertops. A large black-and-white-framed print of the city at night, taken by Calvin, hangs above the sleek black-and-chrome couch. It's my favorite of all the photos he has ever taken. When there is color in the room, it's a pop of red: a pillow or a mah-jongg set that belonged to Calvin's grandmother. We keep our furniture and belongings minimal, so there's lots of open space in our home. Some of our furniture is on wheels, making it easy to rearrange according to desire. I am pleased because I now have a website. I decide to design my website on Squarespace rather than WordPress. The templates on Squarespace are minimalist and modern, designed with photographers, artists, and designers in mind. In them, black-and-white images do not look bare and unpopulated, as I found them to be on WordPress sites. To me, the website I create, with no banners or ads, looks cool and aesthetically pleasing. It's the same way I feel about my uncluttered home.

My partner Calvin is also cool looking. He has almost waist-length black hair, a mustache, and a chin beard, and because of this, from far away, you might think he is Yohji Yamamoto (though Calvin is ethnically Chinese). I wonder if that is part of why I always find him so attractive. He is also not afraid to speak his mind, and on this late summer day, sitting at our kitchen island, after a year of listening to me incessantly talk about this blog I wanted to do, he is clearly out of patience. "Stop with the blah, blah, blah. Just do it!" he groans, his fingers and thumb snapping together repeatedly like a sock puppet telling me to shut up. And that is that. I push his hand aside, stomp to my desk to write an introductory post, and hit publish.

A street photographer, Calvin owns an impressive collection of film cameras. His preferred film and printing processes are black and white. We are yin and yang: he is analog, I am digital. He still uses a flip phone. His concession to digital photography is his purchase of a Leica Monochrom camera. Since I need digital photos for my project, our decision to shoot and post in black and white is accidental too. Being a film photographer, he does not own Photoshop, so retouching wrinkles, even if he were tempted to do so, is not an option. My photos come straight from the camera. This explains the plastic garbage bag or cigarette butt sometimes found next to an elegant Italian leather boot. The photos, like street photography, are real and of the moment.

Because I am a social worker and Calvin is a street photographer, we are not afraid to go anywhere. I am fascinated by the darker side of life. As we walk the East Village, I am reminded of what it was in the 1980s and early '90s when I visited tattoo parlors before they were legal, drank in seedy bars, and had friends who lived in squats. I feel all the attraction/repulsion that goes with transgression. I think this fascination comes from being young during a time when we hid under desks during air raid drills. In Catholic school they warned us about being buried alive and tortured by the "Communists." On TV we watched a *Twilight Zone* episode about the barren life after a nuclear disaster. My granddaughter's modern version is school shootings, active shooter drills, and lockdowns.

As a child, I became tired of being afraid. Rather than withdraw, I embraced the fear and began my lifelong habit of managing terror by studying the object creating it. I would find out everything about it and transform it into an object of interest rather than dread. I furthered this skill when I studied for my first graduate degree in criminal justice at age twenty-two. I visited prisons and hospitals for the criminally insane, and listened to forensic interviews with serial killers. This ability to view the darker side of life neutrally and to transform frightening stories and events into objects of curiosity rather than terror enabled me to go on to practice social work for forty-five years. That approach has been crucial during my work in courts as an expert witness with a specialty in child sexual abuse; it has saved me from becoming so consumed with the terror of horrible events that I can't find the resilience and courage often found in the aftermath. It has shown me the way the most awful events can recede and leave seeds that may grow into something beautiful, something called post-traumatic growth. It has let me see the light in people who have done the most terrible deeds. It has helped me accept my own fear, the losses I have experienced, the pain I have felt, the sins I have committed. This acceptance of lightness and dark gives me eternal hope.

Life is like a garment from an Alexander McQueen collection, something beautiful in its horror. I have always been able to climb up from darkness and feel "the unbearable lightness of being." Perhaps this explains why I'm not so afraid of being old, the changes happening to my body, and dying. Maybe it explains why I always act as though my life is just beginning. Maybe this is why I choose to wear only black and white these days. Can clothes be that powerful, that they can hold such oppositions? Is that why I wanted to study fashion as I approached sixty? Because of its incredible power to contain beauty and/or deterioration?

Roland Barthes, philosopher and author of *The Fashion System*, has explored how clothing concerns all of the human person, not just the body but also the relationships that individual body has with the world. Since studying fashion, it has become clear to me how sociologically important clothing is. This answers the question I am repeatedly asked: What do social welfare and fashion have in common? Fashion documents individual and societal histories and contains and plays with elements of oppression and liberation. For women in particular, it tells stories of how the wearer relates to power and how a woman might manage ambivalence. More and more, I realize that my ever-evolving choice of clothing and the ongoing development of my personal style are about containing the darkness and light of my transaction with the world, as a woman growing older.

Of all the women, young and old, in the blogosphere, I am unique in my stark self-presentation. No retouching, no filters. Looking back now, I wonder whether that's what has really made me stand out. In my photos, through the way I dress, my unsmiling demeanor, my sunglasses, my not-classic beauty, my wrinkles, my white hair, and my presence among the detritus of the streets of the city, I project an attitude that implies a blasé response to the world around me, a cool nonchalance. I am calmly demanding my right to self-creation on my own terms. I couldn't care less if you like me or not, want me or not. I appear unafraid of being old. This is a breath of fresh air for those of all ages seeking the freedom to self-create in a world defined by standards of youth and beauty set amid the backdrop of a multimillion-dollar beauty industry that is waging a never-ending war against getting old.

I did not intend my blog to give style advice or tell women how they should dress. Throughout the years, when asked to style others, I have respectfully declined. I would be a massive failure at it. My version of personal style is just that:

personal. No one can tell you what to wear except you. Embracing your personal style, whether expressed through what you wear or how you live your life, helps you construct a self. The reality one faces when performing stories inspired by fashion is that we are performing in the context of living our real life. This helped me evolve my style to meet the challenge of making inspirational clothing functional for the everyday roles and tasks of women. You tell a story through the clothes, the haircut, the accessories that you wear, the objects you surround yourself with, the places you go, the time you live in, the geography of where you live, and the choices you make.

In designing my platform, I was purposeful in that I did a lot of research and I read fashion theory. Yet at the same time I was improvisational. There were many lucky accidents along the way. Creating something new and not seen before seems to come from something intuitive in you; it's about what you've read, what you know, and how you absorb culture. The luck part of it is that you're putting yourself out at just the right time, letting whatever happens happen, and that's what I feel happened to me. That was my lucky accident. I hit the cultural scene just after the bloggers who came before me had challenged all the rules about fashion and who should be part of it. They made cracks in the wall that people like me, an ordinary woman with an interesting life, could squeeze through to find our way in.

Rules about fashion, or what you should wear at any age, are irrelevant when it comes to personal style. That's the attitude I convey in my photos, and what I choose to write about. It is the genesis of my hashtag, #AgeIsNotAVariable. We do not all age the same. We each have our own style. How we are old is a unique and very personal experience. Some of us are lucky and others are not. Our thoughts, behaviors, feeling states, genetics, culture, and social identities like gender, race, ability, sexual orientation, and class are the materials we have to work with. Systems of power that discriminate, excluding some and privileging others, all exert an influence on how we might "style" and "wear" our older life. Like personal style, aging is an individual transaction between a mind, a body, and the context you are living in.

While a fan of most things black and white, I really dislike black-and-white thinking. I like to hold and play with those tensions that make life so gray and delicious. I am both old and young. Although my body may age, I experience myself as a young person full of life on the inside. Each day I meet and work with young people who are brilliant, cool, savvy about how to negotiate the world, and they inspire me. After some hard challenges, they tell me they feel "old." Some identify themselves as "old souls."

The most fun has been developing the persona of the Accidental Icon. She is me and not me. Therein lies the joy and potential of being her. I soon discovered when I put my blog into that world that there are lots of women like her. Loving fashion, having an enjoyment of style as an expression of your authentic identity, your response to the cultural moment and who you are or wanted to be, has no age.

This raises a question about my popularity: Is it really about fashion embracing older consumers, or is it about valuing those individuals who have the capacity to adapt, remain relevant, and be comfortable with experimentation, reinvention, and an interest in culture and the world they live in? These are the folks who know what to make of a lucky accident when one happens to them. Perhaps it's really not about age but about feeling starved by superficiality and wanting a big helping of something or someone that will "stick to our bones like a hearty meal." Perhaps individuals who can close one door with great satisfaction and open another with eager anticipation are simply more interesting. Perhaps those are the people we should try to have in our lives.

62

Weave a Web of Connections

While I like the option of online buying, I prefer the experience of walking into a brick-and-mortar store. Because of the role clothing plays in my performance of life, the experience of going into a beautifully designed space, "being" with clothes, and "improvising" with the people who make and sell them all conspire to create a scene. I fill myself up with experiences and people that combine haphazardly with my DNA, my memory, my subconscious, and my body. These interactions spill out as a photo or a post on my blog. In these spaces I reach out and feel all of fashion's different textures, listen to its music, smell its perfume, and taste all its spices. I have meandering conversations with other people who inhabit this world with me, people who later become my friends.

Dover Street Market is such a store. It is the brainchild of Rei Kawakubo and Adrian Joffe, the couple who lead Comme des Garçons. Inspired by Kawakubo's love of bazaars and an inspirational vision of "beautiful chaos," the Dover Street Market stores are a living bricolage of layers, textures, installations, and tiny stores within stores. They can be found in cities that are considered to be the fashion capitals of the world. The experience of walking in is akin to falling down the rabbit hole. They mix the clothing up, men's with women's. Perfumes appear next to sneakers. There is a mix of CDG lines, luxury designers like Prada and Thom Browne, "unknown designers," and streetwear lines like Supreme. It is in this space that the net of emerging Chinese designers first caught my eye.

Twice a year, Dover Street Market closes for a few days. This is to enable *tachiagari*, or "beginning," a respite that provides an opportunity for new seasonal collections and installations to be born. It also gives the current crop of designers and brands an opportunity to reinvent their individual spaces within the store. Each designer can create their unique space independent of what the other designers might envision.

This has become my frequent haunt, though it is in an unlikely place for a clothing store. It's off the beaten track of Madison Avenue or SoHo, in a small neighborhood populated primarily by Indian restaurants and spice stores. There is no signage. It is so unlike what you would expect a clothing store to be. Sometimes I'm on my way there and I forget how to find it. The eight floors of the store are nested in a gray stone building that used to be the New York School of Applied Design. Sometimes I leave weighed down with many bags. Sometimes I leave with none. I travel light, carrying only the inspiration that springs from engaging visual and social stimulation.

On one visit to the Market, I look for a cropped cotton jacket to go with an apron I wear today. The apron is blue with white polka dots worn over a long white shirtdress. I wear white platform sandals by a designer named Xiao Li purchased for 50 percent off before the last *tachiagari*. By this time, most of the staff know me, and I them—young fashion designers, painters, illustrators, photographers, fashion merchandizers, and stylists, all aspiring like me. They have stories to tell and want to hear mine. I easily end up spending hours there, as I do today. The conversations usually start with me admiring something they are wearing. They might compliment me on what I wear or a particular garment I decide to try on. And then? Unpredictable, just like what's happening with Accidental Icon.

Today a young painter asks to take a photo of my long Ann Demeulemeester skirt, as it exactly combines pink, purple, and gray tones, a pastel color he is looking to re-create in a painting. He tells me that he designs a fashion line with his brother. As the conversation unfolds, it turns out he also uses performance art to engage people in hard conversations and works with not-for-profits to do so. I am reminded of when I did the same in the late 1990s. We weave our discussion with threads from the worlds of fashion, art, performance, social welfare, and justice. There are multiple patterns and intersections. We make a date to have tea to see where further talk may lead us. It's the far-ranging discussion I might expect to have in my university but that I rarely engage in with my colleagues in this era of specialization. What might it say about the worlds I walk in that I'm having the conversations of my academic dreams and meeting strangers who fire every neuron in my brain in Rei Kawakubo's "temple of fashion," Dover Street Market? Sometimes a conversation can be the greatest adventure of your life.

When I remember the early years of Accidental Icon, my fondest recollections are of how meeting new people and transacting with different fashion spaces provided shape to who the persona Accidental Icon and I were becoming. Fashion exerts its influence not only on the physical world but also on the thoughts, feelings, and behaviors of human beings. The physical world and the effect of humans influence fashion. During these interactions, I am influenced by culture. I influence culture.

In his book *Being a Character*, the British analyst Christopher Bollas suggests that we all have an idiom for our own life and self that healthy adults continue to develop throughout their lifespan. We do this uniquely by always looking out for "objects" (places, people, or things) of interest to transact with. He calls these objects "evocatively nourishing." Is that phrase not just delicious? In looking for my objects, I pay close attention to the parts of me that feel restricted, the parts of me that feel small. I discover that different people and places bring out different parts of me, so I learn to ask, What are the parts of me that are straining to get bigger, to burst out of my chest? How might that help me target the people I want to meet and the spaces where I need to go?

Digital systems are social and interactive and therefore potentially increase how people exert influence and power. My success with them is a case in point. My experience tells me that this digital arena is where important conversations take place, where new notions of change may rise and occur, where lucky accidents may happen. In this time of uncertainty and fast movement in technology, there are wide-open spaces of the not-yet-known. One can wait and see what emerges or be the one who creates something that fills it in.

Instagram and my blog are my digital Dover Street Market. I am inspired by the visuals I find on Instagram during this time, before it has come to be about selling, videos, or Stories. It is about beautiful images that creative people want to share. While I am meeting new people and developing fashion friends in real life, I am also meeting them here. Because of Instagram, I begin a treasured friendship with a woman my age who lives in Australia. We share the common experience of being two of the more notable "hip and cool" older women on the platform, bemused and amused by what's happening to us. We both eventually get modeling contracts. Despite its digital origin, we use our relationship to keep us both real and grounded. Eventually we meet in real life, share brunch in the West Village, have dinner together in Harlem with our partners, plan a trip to Japan. Using WhatsApp, we still speak frequently, arrange to meet in London. It is now nine years since the first time our images crossed each other's digital paths.

My interaction with others and a place more usually occurs first in real time and then transforms into an idea or thought that I express in a digital conversation. I pose a question. More people join and expand the discussion in unpredictable ways. Some strands of the conversation are dropped; others are picked up. When they join, I send each follower a rose emoji. In these early days, when followers trickle onto my platform, a handful every day, I see them as partners in an ongoing discussion. In this way, they are still real people to me. Some, like my friend from Australia, I will meet in the analog world. The more I post, the more I blog, the more I understand that the work of understanding systems and networks happens through asking myself and my followers the question "What kinds of conversation is it important to have now, and with whom should we be having them?"

As I venture more into the spaces of fashion, I find that it is more than just the clothes or designers I admire. It is a system of many interconnected parts. The fashion system embraces the craftsmanship and the commerce aspects. It includes the production of clothes and also their consumption. The fashion system reveals the entire cycle of a garment, from start to finish. *System* in the broadest definition is a network of interacting people and the environment they are interacting in. Despite the democratization of fashion by social media, gatekeepers, rules, and relations of power still control the system.

As a newbie I lurk on the periphery, learning the rules and norms of this new system I find myself in. Perhaps I might better understand how to challenge some of them. I remind myself of the wisdom that my seam-ripping professor shared: there is more than one way to reach a destination. Even when I was locked outside the gate, I carefully observed and noted the details of this world of fashion to understand how I might take part, until I found the tiny opening where I could insert a crowbar, widen it, and squeeze myself in.

In 2015 I am still far from runway shows and fashion weeks; even farther from seats in the front row. Still, I want to find some way to participate. That's when I discover through an ad in *Women's Wear Daily* that one way I can pseudo-explore Fashion Week is to use my blog to get a press pass to market shows. I fill out the application, not expecting to get a pass, as I am still quite unknown. Much to my surprise, I receive my credentials for my very first show: Tranoi. It will be held in a former nightclub in Chelsea, the Tunnel. Market shows are ways for brands to showcase their work and attract the attention of buyers for clothing stores and boutiques. In New York and Paris, they follow the runway shows. The "real" fashion press doesn't attend them, which explains why an unknown like me is able to get a pass.

While there may be an established brand or two, most of the designers here are just beginning their careers. I spend hours meeting and talking to designers. It's a surprise that some recognize me as Accidental Icon and exclaim that they follow me. Busy buyers rarely stop, so for the designers it means three long days of sitting and waiting to pique someone's interest. They are grateful to have anyone stop and ask them about their work, even if you are not buying. They are lyrical as they tell me about their inspirations and share the stories they want to tell about their collection. One designer tells me she imagines her beautiful pieces hanging on the store racks as if they are sleeping beauties. To her, they have no function, no movement, no life, until someone makes them their own. Each person's style is the kiss that awakens the garment, making it so much more than something that hangs in a store.

The market shows are where I generate fresh content for my blog. No one else wears the clothes emerging designers gift me, so I have a highly unique wardrobe. Most have spent every dime they have just producing their clothes, so have no budget for PR. These designers help me build my platform, and because I love their clothes and kiss them awake, I help them build their brand. My blog readers care about and want to hear a designer's personal story. Later my new friends take me to the garment district, where I meet patternmakers, learning about tech packs and how clothing is actually manufactured. I experience the whole of the fashion system, not just a small part of it.

Most of the designers I speak with have strong values related to sustainability and view their clothes as pieces to be collected and cherished rather than rapidly consumed. For this reason, the fabrics and materials are luxurious, the tailoring and craftsmanship outstanding, and there is innovative construction and use of textiles. You can experience, feel, and touch the clothes and receive pleasure from the beautiful objects that they are. There is a concern with maintaining the DNA of a brand. That means growing at a slower pace, having personal relationships with craftspersons, producers, buyers, customers, and local manufacturers, and keeping a focus on the process of creating. Later those who become successful have runway shows of their own that will appear as slideshows in Vogue Runway. I am invited to sit in the front row. There is something very important to us about mutual support and loyalty.

Interactions in systems may be mutually beneficial, or they can be parasitic and predatory. They can be both at the same time. I find this to be true in the fashion system too. I value these interactions that promote learning and growth, give information and advice, or provide recommendations. These interactions are directed from one person to another, benefiting each, bolstering reputation in an exchange of social capital or knowledge to their individual or mutual advantage. Market shows are the system where Accidental Icon and her new designer friends can flourish—where conversation can later transform into a new essay, or an innovative design for a dress.

Positive social connections are good for our emotional and physical health. When we have meaningful relationships with others, we are more likely to feel that we have a purpose, that we belong and have a place in the world. We feel valued and seen by others, which creates a sense of well-being and counteracts feelings of invisibility. Our levels of anxiety and stress are lower when we are engaged meaningfully with others. Being purposeful about the systems we enter and the networks we form can be where and how we flourish. And that has not a thing to do with our age.

I'm in Shanghai, sitting across the table from the fashion designer Masha Ma. She is a graduate of Central Saint Martins in London, probably the most notable school of fashion design. While there, she assists Alexander McQueen. We are in a café in a small mall close to her studio. It is near the Bund, a street that hugs the curve of the Huangpu River. The Bund is home to Shanghai's richest collection of historical architecture. When darkness falls, you can see the modern Shanghai skyline.

Masha is older than the group of emerging fashion designers, also from Central Saint Martins, I will later meet on this trip. She graduated in 2008. She comments on her education in the "old" Central Saint Martins building, worrying that the new building with its gleaming modern studios, opened in 2011, will not contain the ghosts of rebellion that looked over her shoulder as she cut pattern pieces on the weathered wood tables that McQueen and John Galliano also used in the old one.

Masha's Paris collection this spring features clothes that make women look ready for a fight. Her T-shirts flaunt slogans like "Transgressive Sexual Practice," referencing bell hooks and valorizing resistance against patriarchal norms. Wearing large black-framed glasses and a black sweatshirt that reads "Darth Vader," she speaks with an intensity I recognize in myself. We discuss the importance of the work fashion can do to empower women. It feels like our voices join in a battle cry.

When I remember how I came to be here this day, meeting someone I admire many time zones from home, the word *network* springs to mind. There are several definitions, and many kinds of networks. I suppose they all apply. The one I like today is: "Any netlike combination of filaments, fibers, lines, veins and passages."

In a photo of me in *W Magazine,* I sit on a grand stairway carpeted in emerald green. I am in a menswear atelier in Shanghai. I wear an impeccably tailored brocade smoking jacket. My gray hair is in a roll on the top of my head. I wear jeans and maroon velvet slippers. My blue eyes look straight up into the camera. Underneath them are faint smudges that reveal my jet lag. I circled half the globe to be here. The jacket is a deep midnight blue with a sumptuous mix of blooming pink and purple flowers. They bow their heads from pale green stems. If I could pick one garment to symbolize the lushness of that trip to Shanghai, it would be this silk brocade jacket. Brocade is a complex weave of fibers that creates a richly decorated and ornamental fabric: a network of sorts.

Like a brocade, many strands of encounters would come together on my Shanghai trip to create a rich and textured experience. It began with a Chinese student who found her way from Shanghai to Parsons in New York by way of Central Saint Martins. Her name is Liya, and she directs a creative collective of fashion designers, photographers, art directors, and videographers under the name Cube NYC. We met through another Parsons friend I met on Instagram, who wanted to dress me in her designs as a response to a professor who had made a comment about fashion being for the young. I was happy to join her small rebellion, and agreed to wear her clothes in an editorial for *Sicky* magazine.

After we met, Liya asked if she could make a video about me. All the members of her collective wore Yohji and Comme des Garçons. Ageless clothes make for kindred spirits. It intrigued them to learn that I was a professor. We took some footage at my university. Later, as we traveled through the East and West Village, it looked as though I was surrounded by a flock of crows. We filmed. We talked. We ate dumplings. Drank tea. Shared stories. The last clip of the final video is me with my hands and head thrown up to the sky, full of joy, surrounded by falling leaves. What you can't see are all the folks dressed in black, laughing and throwing leaves in the air to get the shot because there was no wind that day. We are all running into something, faces turned to the sun.

Shortly after we filmed the video, I received an invitation to take part in a conference. I was delirious with excitement. It was a moment of convergence; my professor and influencer selves could both attend. The conference, titled Fashion+Social+Media, was hosted by the USC Annenberg School for Communication and Journalism. The conference featured a panel presentation and a series of experiential events that allowed participants to play with fashion: paper dolls that could be dressed in copies of outfits worn by participating influencers; a "catwalk"; a graffiti wall to pose in front of; large cardboard reproductions of iconic looks from fashion history; a room where one could browse through fashion magazines. The presentation included two panels: one of academics who researched and wrote about digital media, who were there to present their research on social media influencers, and another formed from a diverse group of digital influencers, of which I was one. It was an interesting position to be in; although I am a digital influencer, I am also an academic and a researcher.

The academic panel was presented first. It was an odd sensation for me to be in what we refer to in research as the subject position—the object of research rather than the one conducting the research. The power dynamics of such a relationship became quite clear when I heard myself being represented in ways that did not quite fit with my lived experience. According to the esteemed academics, our primary motivation was to become famous and "known." The host of the event was a skilled interviewer of both panels, and effortlessly exposed the gap that exists between theory and practice—that place where knowledge is reconfigured in its application to real life. What the academics did not identify, but what became clear as some of the influencers spoke, was the pleasure we receive from the process of creative work and the relationships forged with our readers and followers.

So how does this relate to the Shanghai trip, you ask? At the USC conference, several Chinese students from all over the campus, not just in journalism, came to hear me speak. A few months earlier, a famous Chinese influencer, Gogoboi, had written an article suggesting that I could be an aspirational model for modern Chinese women. This resulted in my going viral on Weibo and other Chinese social media platforms. Curious, I asked the students what made me so interesting. Their answer: "You're a mother, a grandmother, a PhD, a professor, and a social media star!" In their view, this meant you could maintain cherished cultural values while embracing modern life and technology too. I was someone they "could bring home to meet their parents," so to speak, when they wanted to argue that a job in social media could be a viable option. The other answer was that some Asian cultures have a different view of older people and what makes a person influential than those in the West.

After the panel, one student came to ask me a question, referring to himself simply as Brown. During the conversation, I mentioned that I was scheduled to go to Shanghai the next month. He told me he lived there, and spontaneously asked if he could be my assistant for the trip. It would be no trouble for him to return home, he said. In some sense, this would be a way for him to get experience performing a role he could potentially have in a future career. He was eager to explore the role of influencer for himself. Knowing no one in Shanghai, not speaking Chinese, and being at the mercy of a busy PR person I had never met, I said, Why not?

I discovered during further discussion that Brown knew Liya, the director of Cube NYC, who also comes from Shanghai. By the time I arrived in China, between the two of them, I had a packed schedule, complete with a personal photographer and a car. The itinerary my new friends made for me, unlike the one I was given by the PR person, would take me into places that only people who live in Shanghai knew. There I would meet interesting people I never would have otherwise had access to. Left to the devices of my overly booked and harried PR person, aside from my contracted work of speaking at Shanghai Fashion Weekend, I would have spent most of my stay in my hotel room or in the surrounding area. I knew not a word of the language. But because I was open to a serendipitous meeting with a fashion design student who wanted to stick it to her professor, a woman in New York who went to Central Saint Martins, and a young student studying communications in California, I had what remains one of the most magical experiences of my life.

The first night I'm in Shanghai, I have dinner with Brown, my new photographer, and a group of young and upcoming fashion designers at a restaurant called Oriental House.

Back home in New York City, I had encountered some of the clothing and accessories produced by these young designers at Dover Street Market: Angel Chen, Percy Lau, ShuShu/Tong, Momo Wang, and the maker of the white sandals I'm wearing, Xiao Li. She is pleased to see them on my feet. All the designers I share this first meal with, like Masha Ma, attended Central Saint Martins in London. In school far from home, they had formed a tight cohort. After graduation, like colorful birds, they flew and landed in Shanghai, on its way to becoming yet another fashion capital of the world. Over bowls and plates of steaming food I've never encountered before, we talk about their work and the network of support they've created for one another here, lasting well beyond graduation. It is the absent member of their cohort—my New York friend Liya, who could not make the trip to join us—who has arranged this dinner.

After the meal, I receive gifts. Brown tells me this is a common practice. Percy Lau presents me with a pair of rimless round sunglasses from her collection. They are the coolest of cool. Momo Wang, the founder of the Museum of Friendship, presses a white linen bag embossed with flowers into my hand. She has filled it with trinkets that signify that I am part of her circle of friends. One pair of earrings are constructed of pieces of rope tied in a knot. One half of another pair, constructed of embroidered cloth, is a hand with a blue gingham sleeve cuff. The other half of the pair is a pointing finger with a heart at the tip. There is a brooch made of interwoven silk threads. It is the same color blue as the brocade jacket I try on and model two days later in the menswear atelier. It hangs in the shape of a net and captures the beautiful memories I have of this dinner and all the new friends I made that night, who are old friends now.

The evening after I present at the Fashion Weekend, I visit the studio of Angel Chen. It is the most colorful room I have ever been in. Angel is playful, full of movement, sharply intelligent, research-oriented, and full of delight about many things and people. Her clothes dance on the line between East and West, as does her fashion experience. She tells me that her father owns a paint company and is an expert at mixing colors, and explains a complex process of shrinking that results in a particular texture of a textile. I am struck by how her playfulness, movement, and intelligence manifest in her designs. When I later wear some pants of her design in an Instagram post, the caption is "Keeping new friends close." Those parts of a new friend that are present in their clothes allow me to have an ongoing relationship with them, whether or not I see them again.

While I've never had a large number of friends, I'm lucky to have friends from my past who remain in my life, including one significant best friend each from childhood, college, my doctoral program, and my work life. They are historians that connect me to my past and, as a group, represent all the important periods of my life. They are the keepers of my secrets; some of them know things that the others do not. Some remember things about me that I have forgotten. When I am with them, they remind me of all the selves I used to be, and the parts of those selves that remain. These are the relationships that can withstand months without contact. They are always there when you can come back to them. They understand that life happens. Friendships are unique relationships in this way, because, unlike family relationships, we choose to enter them.

I have what I call "creative catalyst" friends, those who inspire and help me reinvent when I need to. These relationships seem to come into my life when there is a chasm I must cross between knowing and not knowing. These are the friends who travel with me through becoming. These are the friends who are further along in the process or the skills I am attempting to cultivate in myself, the hands that grab me so I don't fall over the edge, or support me when I am scared to jump. They are my network. They are my net. For me they have been as wide-ranging and varied as the law professor who taught me what it really means to be a teacher who can help students think critically, an artist who taught me how to transform my experience into images and sounds, a younger, more experienced traveler who introduced me to the joys of the voyage, a dance therapist who taught me how to move freely, and all the young designers who taught me about fashion.

For all of my life, my friends have been of all ages. Sometimes they are older than I, and perhaps at those times I require their wisdom and experience. Sometimes, like now, at the beginning of my foray into fashion and social media, they are younger because I need to learn something about the time we are living in, and I require a dose of contagious energy. Like the classes I sit in during my time in fashion school, most of the spaces I travel through as the persona of Accidental Icon is emerging are those where I am the oldest person in the room. These multigenerational friendships have unique benefits. They broaden perspectives, provide role models in both directions, boost energy, and make both parties feel valued. I think the reason I attract people of all ages is that I have a positive view of being old, and a great respect for those who are young. My research confirms it: people with positive expectations about aging make more new friends of all ages and keep them longer. But in reflection, I want to pose this question: Is it really about having positive expectations about being old, or is it simply having positive expectations about yourself and others?

63

Fear Not Risks and Welcome Mistakes

Because I cannot abide being bored, I am forever jumping into new experiences. Often, it's jump first, think later. When there is an inevitable crash and I end up on my ass, my mother used to say, "For someone so smart, you are unbelievably stupid." This was her unvarnished tough-love way of calling me naive. Despite my mother's concern, I have found time and time again that a state of blind fearlessness, especially when beginning a new adventure, has its merits. Being naive indicates that you have a kind of optimism about the world, an expectation that good will come your way. It is an antidote to the unhappiness and inertia that comes with overthinking and overanalyzing. It helps me take a risk I might not otherwise take if I thought too much about what I was about to do. I am not alone in this. I have a friend with a hugely successful sustainable fashion brand who told me, "If I knew when I started what I know now, I probably would not have taken the leap to start my brand."

I have found during my time as Accidental Icon that this trait has worked in my favor. As Accidental Icon, my optimistic innocence has earned me the reputation of being genuine, accessible, and charming. It allows me to forgive myself when I make a mistake. I can tell myself I just wasn't aware. Not knowing how famous someone is makes it more like meeting a new person in a coffee shop and having an impromptu chat. I'm my real self; unguarded, comfortable, and free. The husband-and-wife team of Adrian Joffe and Rei Kawakubo have made one of my favorite fashion brands, Comme des Garçons, a spectacular success. They are always creating things that are new and never seen before. Joffe has no formal training in business, and Kawakubo was never formally trained in fashion design. In an interview in the *Financial Times*, Joffe explains why this lack of training has actually worked for the brand: "I think sometimes it's easier to break the rules if you don't know what they are." Perhaps not knowing the rules of engagement is what has accounted for my success in the world of fashion as well.

I'm seated at a fashion show. I am early, as is the man sitting next to me. No one sits on either side of us, and I strike up a conversation with him. I tell him how I came to be sitting in the front row. We have a lovely conversation about Fordham, which some of his siblings attended. I find out he is good friends with the designer whose show we are attending, and whose clothes I am now wearing. I ask his name and if he works in fashion. He gives a little smile and says, "Yes, I do. My name is Thom Browne. I'm a designer." In a Getty Images photo from the show, my head cocked next to his before I knew who he was, I look comfortable, as if I belong exactly where I am, in the front row of a fashion show sitting next to a famous fashion designer. I am dressed in a deep-midnight-blue velvet suit embellished with silver spiderwebs. His arm is around my shoulder; we look like old friends. As soon as I realize who he is, I feel like a complete fool, but you'd never know it based on this picture. I try to clean it up by explaining how it was the clothes that I remembered; I would know his anywhere, it was just him I couldn't place. "No worries," he reassures me.

When I first started, failing to recognize certain famous designers or mispronouncing the names of brands created some embarrassing moments. But on that day, believing that Thom Browne was just a charming man wearing shorts in winter and chatting about Catholic schools helped me remain relaxed and real. This produced a lovely, widely circulated photo. However, as in the moments I was at the receiving end of my mother's pithy mantra, there were also times my naiveté got me in trouble and I had to figure out how to clean up the mess.

———

It's the late fall of 2016. Accidental Icon has just celebrated her second birthday. On this day, I enter a cavernous white photo studio in Brooklyn. In my arms is a garment bag holding several articles of clothing. I'm wearing jeans, a Comme des Garçons sweatshirt with a ruffled Adidas stripe that begins at my neck and travels through the midpoint of my shoulders and down the top of my arms, and black Converse high-tops with a CDG PLAY heart logo. I'm very nervous because this is the first time I'm being photographed by someone other than Calvin. I'm walking into a space where I know no one at all. I hand over my bag to a stylist, who hangs the items on a rack. They include a pair of wide-leg Yohji overalls and an embroidered black tulle bomber jacket with black and white stripes around the cuffs. I am introduced to the photographers, a two-person team called JUCO known for their wildly explosive use of color. Somehow I feel it's a mistake that I'm here; all the clothes I brought are black and white. The other models are like walking rainbows.

I'm here in this white cave to do a photo shoot and interview for Refinery29. Each year, the art direction team puts together a calendar that the founders send to all their advertisers and contributors—their creative version of a holiday card. In the colorful end product of this shoot, I am Ms. April. Refinery29 is a New York–based fashion, lifestyle, and commerce site. Four young founders launched it in 2005 with a focus on emerging designers and independent boutiques, and a mission to help readers develop their own personal style. Its Webby Award–winning content resulted in Refinery29 being named *Fast Company* magazine's No. 2 Most Innovative Company in Style. In 2019, Vice Media acquired the site for millions.

I haven't yet figured out that when a brand or other entity asks you to do a photo shoot or feature, you must do your homework and make sure you do some research about them before you arrive. It seems rather funny in retrospect that for the last thirty-five years, I've been teaching students and the staff I supervise how to meticulously prepare for a first session with a client. Most likely I haven't applied that knowledge to this project because I'm still seeing everything to do with my blog as a lucky accident.

Many people don't believe I'm actually very shy. It's very uncomfortable for me to have my picture taken. To give myself courage, I insist on wearing sunglasses and not smiling. These two small assertions allow me to do what I most appreciate about being the Accidental Icon: go way outside my comfort zone and put myself on the line. Whether I am obeying the mark a famous photographer gives me on the rare occasion I am working with someone other than Calvin or marching along the catwalk in a runway show, I find the spotlight absolutely terrifying and distinctly unpleasant.

Yet what I resolutely place on the decision-making scale is whether this discomfort is worth the price of not trying something at all. As I look back on my life, I have found regret an unproductive emotion and one I try to avoid, because there is nothing I can do about the past. Regret is a kind of fruitless longing for a missed opportunity, a desire for something more. When it comes to how I choose to live my life, I try to make space for what I desire. There are times that is possible and times it must be put aside. I consider desire and its satisfaction seriously these days because of the way life seems to press itself urgently against me. Although I might suffer discomfort while going on fresh adventures, satisfying my curiosity, feeling the rapture when seeing the product of my ever-increasing creative impulse, or expanding my world, this all makes that scale tip in favor of the pleasures of terror. I manage this fear as I manage other dark moments of life: as an object of interest to be observed. Because of this approach I find that the pounding heart and sweaty hands that accompany a state of panic are thankfully a transitory state.

———————————

On the Refinery29 set, the hair and makeup folks, the stylists, both photographers, and the person who later interviewed me are complimentary, professional, and encouraging of fun. Everyone seems over the top in their enthusiasm. The team decides on the bomber jacket because at least the embroidery features pops of red. Maybe I'm projecting, but I can feel a sense of disappointment from this crowd because of my undying loyalty to black and white. I move through the experience feeling unsure, anxious, and, yes, terrified.

It's my turn to be photographed. I wait while those behind the camera debate the right color for the background. Assistants hoist the background up onto the stand, pull it over the floor, and set up the lights. I stand in the middle of a sea of bright turquoise. The photographers keep encouraging me to smile and move freely. I do neither. It feels like hours before they decide they have a photo they like. My face feels so tense and stiff, it probably looks like I just had a facelift. Another photographer will later teach me the trick of stretching my mouth as wide as I can between takes to relax the tension that always seems to accumulate around my lips. I have more fine lines than most around my mouth from all those times I've struggled to keep it shut. In the photo they ultimately choose, I'm in profile, hands upturned and in the air as if I am protecting myself from glaring light. It was probably my reaction to all that color.

I consider the aftermath of panic a kind of free zone, one where I don't have to do any work, where I can eat whatever I want and just relish in the glorious release of the tension and anxiety leaving my body, the luxury of a quiet mind. In the aftermath, images slowly emerge like a Polaroid photo, and memory becomes accessible. In the aftermath, curiosity returns, and I lazily type something in a search box. In the aftermath, I can remember the minor details that did not register during the panic and, with a groan, identify the mistakes I made. I appreciate the catharsis and reflection of this mental habit, the chance to discover all the exciting opportunities that lurk on the periphery. The quote from my interview for this shoot that ultimately lands on my photo as Ms. April is: "I'm taking more risks now than when I was younger. You don't need a script for your life. I've always improvised." I sure as hell did that day.

It's the Monday after the photo shoot. As I reflect on the experience, I recall the presence of a young woman who seemed to be everywhere. She was short like I am. I found her intriguing. She had a nose ring and wore a varsity jacket with sparkling sequined appliqués. Because of her enthusiasm and casual, easy demeanor, I immediately pegged her as an intern. Her presentation was that of being in service to those who were working to make this production possible. Noting how nervous I was, she asked me what kind of music I liked for the shoot, and being in the throes of terror, I looked at her like a deer in headlights. I could not for the life of me pull something from my brain. I finally mumbled, "Rolling Stones." She found some and blasted it. She started dancing like crazy, probably in the hopes that I would too. I did not. I asked her for a glass of water instead.

I remember now that as I was in hair and makeup, being photographed and interviewed, she was always there in my peripheral vision. I realize now that it was she consulting with the photographers, and they consulting with her. It was she who approached and generously offered to take my picture for use on my Instagram. Something, of course, I should have thought of and didn't. She flipped quickly through my account and then produced photos using my iPhone that are among some of my all-time favorites. I spontaneously yelled, "You really get me!" Her casual response: "Well, I looked at your Instagram." I asked her for her card, thinking that as an intern, she might be looking to have other experience. I also said, "Wow, what a great opportunity for someone starting out to work for a company like this."

Later as I reflect on the experience, I google Refinery29. With intensifying horror, I realize that the woman I mistook for an intern is none other than the brilliantly talented executive creative director and cofounder of Refinery29, Piera Gelardi. As creative director, she oversees all visual strategy and execution for the site, including branding, design, art direction, photography, video, and casting. The best adjectives to describe her are ebullient, colorful, creative, vivacious, and over-the-top. There is an aspirational component to the art direction and vision of the site, yet it remains eminently accessible. It is quirky, provocative, and fun, just as she is. She sure knows how to tell a visual story.

As I read about Gelardi's awards and see all the accolades that appear under her name on the web, my stomach sinks, and I cringe at the mistake I have made. People I tell gasp in horror at the gravity of the error. They all seem to know who she is. I am certain that I will never book with Refinery29 again. I have turned off a veritable fountain of opportunities. After fretting for a day or two, I decide to write a blog post, poking fun at myself and owning my mistake. I say I want to be her when I grow up. I list Piera's achievements and suggest that maybe it is I who needs to be her intern. I ask her to reserve me a space in a future crop of interns. I send a link to the post in an email, thanking her for the opportunity. Her response is warm, and it is clear that she appreciates the humor and irony in my post.

I like to think it was that blog post that led to the many opportunities I later had with Refinery29. I appeared in several features, including one for Coach, wearing a varsity jacket. There is an especially charming one that featured my granddaughter and me. I did several interviews, and other times they asked me to comment on various topics. One of the most satisfying opportunities was my inclusion in a short film by Pamela Romanowsky, *Watching You Watching Me*, part of Refinery29's Shatterbox Anthology, an award-winning short-film series dedicated to spotlighting the voices of female filmmakers and providing emerging and established talent the opportunity to realize their vision. The film explores perception, judgment, and the feeling of "otherness." In the film, my "otherness" was being old. This experience made me truly understand the potential of social media in the service of social justice work. If I had written an academic article about ageism or the other isms experienced by those in the film with me, it would be in a journal and read by maybe two hundred people. By telling a story in a film featured on a site like Refinery29, I put it in front of a million pairs of eyes the minute it went up.

Perhaps one of the most important lessons I have learned in my life is how to handle making a mistake. As a young professional in my thirties, I was the director of a residential treatment program for adolescent girls, responsible for twenty troubled young lives and an equal number of staff. I lived in a constant state of anxiety that I would make a mistake, miss something critical. Someone would die or be seriously hurt. The stress of this mindset is unsustainable. I was fortunate to have a supervisor who, to my chagrin, rather than comfort me, wryly remarked that I was being very grandiose to think I had so much control. She taught me that the vast majority of mistakes are fixable. In this way she did provide me with a great amount of comfort. Mistakes are perhaps the most powerful teachers, if one takes ownership of them. Mistakes are opportunities.

I now understand that mistakes are like old clothes: most times they can be mended. I learned in my vintage store class that a seam ripper is also used to remove unwanted stitches from fabric. It allows you to correct mistakes and undo stitches without damaging the textile. In most cases you would never know a mistake had been made. With the right attitude and level of self-acceptance, you can have what I like to call "redoes," where you try something again, this time with the wisdom of learning from the mistake you made before.

I always told my students that mistakes are opportunities to take yourself to a new level of practice, a new level of relationship with the people you work with, if you own them and make your clients aware that you do. This level of honesty is what creates trust. After teaching a class, I would reflect on how it went. At times I would identify moments when I misspoke, responded in a less-than-helpful way to a student comment, or did not intervene in an unproductive student interaction. I made a practice of beginning each class with a reflection about the one before. I would share my "mistakes" and offer other options of what I could have said, could have done, that would have been more helpful. I asked the students to do the same after each class and after each time they met with a client. Brainstorming about what could be done differently became a way for us to come up with innovative solutions that could be deployed in a future scenario. It allowed us to laugh at ourselves, to have humility. With a little creativity, a dose of self-respect, trust, and a sprinkle of humor, a mistake can turn into opportunities you might never have imagined.

———————————

When I hear the word *slouching*, it reminds me of two spectacular women. The first is my grandmother, who always told me not to. The second is Joan Didion and her book of essays *Slouching Towards Bethlehem*. I had a real affinity toward Joan Didion when I was a young woman, and I met her again as an older one when we both appeared in major fashion magazines. Her fashion debut at age eighty came in a Céline ad, and mine in an ad for Valentino. The photos we appear in picture us from the waist up and dressed in black sweaters. She wears an oversize gold pendant; I wear large vintage hoops. Both of us have our hair cut in chin-length bobs. Oversize sunglasses are the star of both ads. Young fashion bloggers like to post our photos side by side. In this moment, it seems that if a woman of a certain age is smart, wears designer eyewear, and does not smile, young women just might aspire to being old. No one was calling us "cute," the form of address usually applied to older women cavorting on the web. The word most often used to describe us was *cool*.

As I look at those photos, I remember an essay Joan Didion wrote, "On Self-Respect." In it, Didion states that people who have self-respect also have character—that which she defines as "the willingness to take responsibility for one's own life." It is self-respect that allows us to take risks, to do the things that are uncomfortable, the things we do not want to do. It is this trait that lets us make mistakes and take something positive from them rather than wallow in regret. It is this trait that allows us to make something we want more than just a romantic notion. Rereading the essay reminds me of all the possibilities and hazards I felt the first time I read it. Looking back, I see I did listen to my grandmother. I do not slouch. Not when it comes to my posture, or in living my life. Head high and back straight, I walk right into the unknown.

Somehow an open casting call found its way to my inbox. It said only that a brand was casting for an eyewear ad, and if interested, I should show up at Tompkins Square Park at 11:00 a.m. on a Saturday. We paraded around in a line while the casting director took notes and her assistant gathered email and phone numbers. They informed me I was in, and told me to wait for an email with more instructions. That night the email appeared, saying I would take part in a very short video for which I would receive $50. I would receive more if they ended up using any photos of me in the ads. They included instructions on where to meet the next day. I was to dress in my usual style. I still did not know the name of the brand, as often they keep these things hush-hush. Later, when I had agents who would not entertain the possibility of my participation without knowing full details like brand and budget, we would have to sign an NDA to get this information.

The café where we were to meet was on the Lower East Side, below Chinatown and near the Manhattan Bridge. I was by myself and sat down at a table with three other models, one a girl with curly blond hair, the others a set of twins with cat's-eye glasses and long dresses. A production assistant checked me in. They offered us coffee, and we waited. As I was beginning to learn, waiting is something you do a lot of during fashion shoots. I was wearing a cropped black mohair sweater underneath a biker jacket, wide-leg Junya Watanabe black trousers with a very fitted butt, high-heeled black boots, and, of course, my signature shades. The assistant returned with a clipboard and asked us to sign some sort of agreement. I signed after skimming. I don't take time with the fine print.

At some point, a different assistant came to collect me. I followed her down the block and across the street and was escorted up the steps into an old tenement building. I had the same sensation I get when I walk through Chinatown and am stopped on the street by someone selling counterfeit designer bags. If I agree to view their wares, they might lead me down the street and into a building. I climb steep steps, go through curtains, and find myself in a hidden room filled with bags and accessories. Along the journey, it's impossible to ignore the possibility that perhaps this is some sort of trap and I will get robbed, as will the designers whose bags are in the room. I recall having this same feeling as I followed the assistant that day.

I entered a large room. This time there were racks of clothes, trays of sunglasses laid out on tables, hair and makeup people. It was clear that the brand I was working for was Valentino. With a shock I recognized the notorious fashion photographer Terry Richardson, known for his oversize aviator glasses, large mustache, and edgy captures of celebrities in mundane, everyday scenes, sitting at the far end of the room in front of a computer. There were whispers at the time of sexual exploitation of his models. I watched him like I was the hawk, not him.

An older woman, dressed in a black cotton coat over black shirt and pants, and black ballet slippers, tortoiseshell reading glasses hanging from her neck, gave me a quick look up and down. She took my arm and brought me over to a man whose head was bent over some papers. He looked up at our approach. I later identified him as Pierpaolo Piccioli, the creative director of Valentino Maison. She looked at him and said with an Italian accent, "What do you want?" It was clear in the interaction that they had worked together a long time. "I like what she has on," he said, "but let's try the skirt." When later asked about why he chose everyday people, all different, all walking around the city for this campaign, he responded, "I don't like the intolerance, giving people boxes to stay in. I like the freedom of being whoever you are." According to *Otticanet Magazine*, an eyewear trade publication that featured this campaign, I was specifically picked because "she embodies the true spirit of the collection: a beauty in a precarious equilibrium between the past and the future, taking its strength from imperfections." I'll take this as a compliment.

From the rack, the stylist's quick and sure hand pulled a long bottle-green-and-black-striped sequined skirt. It was a garment I would die and go to heaven for, but Valentino was way above my pay grade. Today I'd have to wear and return. We went to the tray of sunglasses. The frames she picked were black Lucite layered on a transparent background with a gold bridge and black lenses. I pulled on the skirt; she brought me over again for inspection. He nodded. Makeup refreshed my bright red lip, and they told Terry Richardson I was ready. By now, it was nighttime.

There were four of us: the photographer, his assistant, a production assistant, and me. Terry and I talked about what it was like to be out at night in New York City on the Lower East Side when you were young. I was taken back in time to when I was in high school, taking the train to the Fillmore East to see my idol Grace Slick. I remember being high and waiting on line to get into CBGB in the late 1970s. You could stumble upon Lou Reed and Laurie Anderson on their way to a show. I felt, once again, like I was traveling through the night life, chasing new desires and searching for secrets. There was always some vaguely articulated danger. I felt feverish, lit up by a neon light we passed as we walked. I was unaware my photo was being taken as I remembered. Terry said, "That's it, we've got it." We headed back. My body felt tired, like a morning after, though I also felt kind of beautiful.

About two months later, another email arrived. They had decided to use my videos and photo. They would send me a check for $1,550. I was still naively unaware of what this actually meant. Use them for what, I wasn't sure. I was excited and pleased that they'd chosen me. I heard nothing more, however, and so I moved on.

It was Christmas, and I was excited to spend it with my granddaughter. Now she was two and a half. This would be the first time she had some awareness that there was something special in the air. There would be presents. The new year would bring a number of firsts for us both.

Spring/summer collections and ads usually appear in fashion magazines beginning in January. That's when Valentino's 2017 Glamgloss Eyewear Collection made its debut. My phone blew up as I got texts and emails from friends with screenshots of me appearing in all their favorite fashion magazines. Calvin and I passed high-end eyewear boutiques and saw floor-to-ceiling posters of me in their windows. I felt excited and happy. I did not know that I had been taken advantage of in terms of what I was paid. When it came to the world of fashion, I was still a neophyte, with much more to learn. I was particularly naive when it came to the business aspect of things, since to me what I was doing had nothing to do with a business. I would eventually need an agent to teach me about that. Financial savvy was not a topic taught in social work curriculum, nor was it something I learned from my working-class family. For me the intangible aspects of my new career, like being creative and meeting new people, were far more interesting than the tangible benefits of money or fame. Each experience was as fresh and exciting as this shoot had been. I was still rather clueless about the fact that I could actually make a living from something that was so much fun. I was learning my way around this fascinating new world, one mistake at a time. Because of how I usually respond to them, fortunately none of my early mistakes were catastrophic. In fact, some of them turned out to have payoffs I did not anticipate or could have ever imagined. Especially this one.

In March another email appeared in my inbox. Apparently the exposure I received from being in the eyewear campaign had brought me to the attention of an agent who worked at a well-regarded international modeling agency, Elite. In her email she asked if I was represented, and if not, would I be open to a call. She told me that if she had been representing me, she would have negotiated something like $50,000 for what I just did for Valentino. I found this unbelievable; that was more than half my yearly salary as a professor with decades of experience and a PhD, for a few hours' work. I could hear my mother's voice yelling the word *stupid* in my ear.

Never believing in a million years that a modeling contract or that kind of money would ever come from what I was doing with my blog and consignment store clothes, I listened to what the agent had to say. I liked the vision she presented, and that she seemed to understand me. She knew I didn't really want to be a model. Her plan was to develop me as a "personality." At the end of the call, I ended up with a modeling contract. Two weeks later, my new agent got me another international campaign to make up for the Valentino one. So even though I was naive and clueless, once again, it was taking risks and screwing up that led me to my next set of adventures and took me all over the world. While I was not paid what I should have been for my work with Valentino, it had given me international exposure, brought me to the attention of an agent at a top modeling agency, and resulted in a plethora of lucrative opportunities. This was a mistake worth making. Mistakes, while sometimes quite painful, with terrible consequences—I don't want to minimize that fact—can also be of great value. It's all about how you handle them when they inevitably occur, and what you creatively and morally decide to make of them. These days I come to see them as lucky accidents that teach me a lesson I need to learn so that my life may be better.

64

Remain Visible

study the coat before purchasing it. I return to the store to view it over and over. I try it on more than once. Every time, I experience an involuntary sharp intake of breath when I look in the mirror and see myself wearing it. The coat differs from most of my usual tailored black-and-white selections. It's not something I would usually wear. It borders on outrageous, and I can't see wearing it in my everyday life. But I've learned to listen to my breath when it tries to tell me something. Despite my hesitation, I bring it home.

The coat is oversize and folds around me like a box. It's white silk and printed with large, juicy red lips. They appear smeared and swollen, as if they have been kissed over and over. The word *erotic* comes to mind. There is something compelling about a gash of red lipstick against the palest of white. A shirt collar, a face. Perhaps that is the reason the only lipsticks I own are in shades of red. I wear the coat to Central Park during a snowstorm. Calvin and I are here hoping to enjoy the snow and get photographs for my blog. I need more content to have in reserve. I am busy traveling: LA, Lisbon, Madrid, and London. We aren't able to roam around the city doing our own photo shoots as often as we'd like. I miss Calvin being the one who takes pictures of me, now that I'm working with other photographers. I'm still teaching full-time too. In the photo we eventually capture, the white of the coat blends into the snow. It appears I am covered in messy kisses.

The red lips against the white of the coat and snow remind me of the face of a geisha. When the background is white, everything else stands out in sharp detail and becomes clearer. When doing research about why geishas paint their face white, I discovered several theories. One is that the practice began during a time when there was not enough light at night during a geisha's performance. They painted their face white and lips red, making their facial expressions visible even in the dimness of candlelight. The white paint with the contrasting red lip also serves to hide any variance of their facial expressions, so they can always appear happy. In the tradition of Kabuki theater, actors paint this same white makeup on. They add color and line in such a manner that a mask emerges to create the character being performed. There is something in these two identities that speaks to how I feel about my increasing visibility. I want my expressions to be "seen," but I also wish for the safety of a mask as I now perform my life in the public view.

It's been three years since I started the Accidental Icon. I'm receiving more and more attention from the fashion and popular press. My follower count on Instagram exceeds six figures. I am careful in what I reveal, and naively believe I am in control of it. Perhaps I still retain some of the grandiosity my old supervisor told me about. People know I am a professor, I have a partner named Calvin and a daughter and granddaughter who remain nameless, I live in New York City, and I use clothing to express my identity. That is all. There are no cameras allowed or interviews conducted in my home. I continue to enjoy a degree of privacy in my "other life" outside of Accidental Icon. I find I don't like it when another faculty member mentions it, or it comes up in the course of my social work. I feel embarrassed. At the time, I don't think about what this means. I consider myself lucky not to have encountered the trolls or negative comments that other people I follow seem to attract. I want to keep it this way.

I admit I really did not expect, nor wish, to receive all this attention. It's not just me who feels this way. My family and friends share my perception that my fame feels more dream than reality. When I first told my sister I was starting a fashion blog, she rolled her eyes at me. It's very hard to describe, but I experience Accidental Icon as someone who is me, but not me. She is more like a role I play, a performance I am starring in. She is a character I invented as I went along. While this part of me heads to the spotlight like a moth to a flame, once I am there, I am not sure I want to be. Perhaps I fear I will be burned, or my wings will be clipped.

Pushing past fears or powerful messages that define us and going against societal constraints is not painless. We all have different access to privilege, which can make it easier or harder. Most times, there is risk involved. The greatest risk is that someone else will hijack the story you want to tell about yourself. While there is something gained, there is also something lost. Following the preference of the notoriously elusive Rei Kawakubo, my aim with Accidental Icon has always been that people "get to know me through my clothes." What I choose to wear, how it inspires me, and how I write about that choice is the way I want to tell my story.

I never intended my story to be one about age. My love of clothing and how to style it as an expression of identity is the tale I want to tell. This has nothing to do with how old I am. I still believe this. In 2017 my age began to be a part of the Accidental Icon story. The features written about me all begin and end with my age. It's not just that I have an interesting style that makes me unique; it's that I am sixty-four years old and being stylish. It's not just that I have re-invented myself with a career completely different from the one I already have; it is that I am sixty-four while doing it. While other fashion bloggers receive comments about their new bag or what they wear, my followers comment that I make them feel less afraid of being old. I give them cour-age to take a risk in older life, to disregard someone telling them they are too old to wear something or dye their hair purple if they wish. The world seems incredulous that I am doing what I am doing at the age of sixty-four. I am not fad-ing away or riding off into the sunset. I find it odd that they are making such a big deal about my age; I don't consider it relevant to what I am doing now, or what I wear. It is dur-ing this time that I invent and use the hashtag #AgeIsNotA Variable and add, ". . . when it comes to getting dressed." When asked about my age in regard to what I am doing, I cheekily respond, "I don't comment on that. Just look at my photos, I'm performing it!"

Until that moment, probably because of that naiveté my mother hoped I would outgrow, I never thought of being old as having anything to do with being creative, reinventing yourself, or wearing whatever you damn well please. I must admit I was somewhat surprised by how many women feared becoming invisible and how excited they became watching what has happened to me. So somehow my creative project took a different turn than what I had imagined. It became a story of how to be old.

I believed I could maintain a state of being "invisibly visible" and control my narrative through what I chose to divulge in my posts. My pictures told a story of their own and became a projection of what others wanted to see in them. I guess if you decide to wear a coat with bright, sexy red lips in the middle of a snowstorm and don't think you'll be seen, it may be more of a leap than you believed it to be.

In 2017 a story about my "success," defined by the media as being signed by a modeling agency, was published on the digital platform Bored Panda in an article titled "Journalists Accidentally Confuse a 63-Year-Old Teacher with a Fashion Icon and It Ends Up Changing Her Life." The article got 3.1 million views. Within twenty-four hours of publication, I amassed 300,000 new followers on Instagram. I made a note that 90 percent of them were between eighteen and thirty-five. It was the first time I wasn't able to send every new follower a rose emoji. It was the first time someone else told my story the way they wanted to, not the way I knew it to be true. The adherence to facts was fast and loose. For example, I was sixty-four in 2017, not sixty-three.

A rapid succession of features followed, with similar headlines in the *Washington Post*, *NBC News*, *BuzzFeed*, *InStyle*, and *Huffington Post*. Now there were another 200,000 followers; my Instagram notifications lit up like a yard full of fireflies. Featured prominently in most of the articles was a photo of me hanging off a fire escape in Chinatown. Dare I say, it has become the most shared and iconic photo of me. It's the photo that firmly established my reputation as a badass.

In the photo I wear a garment graciously provided by a friend I met at one of the market shows. People had never seen it before on Instagram or on the internet. It's a strapless black leather gown, worn with a high-necked crop top of gray wool with black flowers. The top made me feel less exposed, the long bell sleeves that look like lambswool revealing only the tips of my fingers. A hairstylist friend of the photographer who took the photo swept my hair up. It looks like a white flame atop my head. I am on fire. Large black hoop earrings complete the look, along with oversize aviator sunglasses. My lips are bright crimson, the color of blood; this is an edgy and dangerous side of red. The makeup artist, a friend of the photographer who is also my upstairs neighbor, perfectly applied the lipstick. By the end of the shoot, it will bleed into the fine lines surrounding my mouth, but for now, you can't see the smudging. There is something about this photo that draws you in. In it, it seems like I am leaning toward the viewer. I look put together, unstoppable, sexy and free. Suddenly, thanks to the dizzying speed of the internet as this photo exploded across the web, my face and body were more visible at sixty-four than they ever were at any other time of my life. That includes even when I was twenty-five, when our culture had decided I was at the peak of my youth and sexual attractiveness.

My blog followers have, from the start, been ardent fans of my writing. My new agent in London suggests I keep a diary. "There will be a book," she divines. I love her. She knows me so well. I ask my followers, "If I were to write a book, what would you like to me to write about?" While I receive a wide variety of topics in response, the one that most frequently appears from women of all ages is "How to not become invisible." A sense of urgency and despair about the topic is palpable. My fans think I've discovered some kind of magic that prevents me from disappearing. My young followers tell me how terrified they are about getting old. Seeing me in that photo is making them think that maybe it's not so bad. Perhaps, they imagine now, we will not have to disappear. As a bonus, they can be a badass like me.

My new fans continue to write to me. From some younger women and those approaching or going through menopause, I hear them express fear about losing their attractiveness and desirability. In the background of the responses is always the question: To what degree do we tie our perceptions of being visible to our feelings about the loss of youth and sexual attractiveness, or our ability to attract a male gaze, or any gaze? There are expressions of grief and frustration when one is no longer perceived as a sexual being. Perhaps these fears are why the photo of me hanging off the balcony, seeming to invite kisses that will smear my red lipstick all over my face, went viral.

The concerns of the women who write to me are as different as their demographics. For some, it is the fear of becoming irrelevant and dismissed. Those older than I have pragmatic reasons for not wanting to be invisible, like "not being bumped into on the street," or being ignored in a store or other place where they want to get service. Some older women rant about the injustice of feeling less valued and treated differently than older men. There are those who suggest that some older women are less valued than *other* older women. Some have experienced themselves as invisible their entire lives, and so this was nothing new. Some weep with gratitude just to have survived long enough to be old. Some reveal that even when they are seen, they are often perceived inaccurately. To this I can relate.

While I was styling a visible life as Accidental Icon, I kept one part of me invisible on purpose. I was in a moment of enormous change, and through that transformation, I kept my ambivalence about my newfound fame to myself. The stress of maintaining my full-time job as a professor; the guilt I feel about missing my mother's ninetieth-birthday party because I was halfway around the world; not seeing my granddaughter enough—I always felt these challenges, and in looking back, I find I struggled with them on my blog. My blog was like a little diary hidden away in a corner of the internet. Only my original followers read it, and still do. By this time, blogs were passé. It was all about Instagram. Visuals only, no words. Outside only, not inside.

More and more, the persona of the badass visible in my photos was the only person I felt I could share publicly. There was pressure to always live up to it. In all sincerity, I just could not comprehend what was so special about me. While I knew I had a good deal of self-acceptance and self-respect, I did not feel like a badass twenty-four hours a day. I did not see in myself what other people saw in me to make this unbelievable turn of events happen, to explain why I received thousands of emails and comments from women of all ages thanking me for changing their lives. My agents and the people I worked with found this reticence to be confusing. In my mind I was just living my life as I always had, reinventing, learning something new, and engaging in stimulating conversations. I did not see what was so special about it. I had not yet come to fully understand that it was because I was doing these things when I was old that others thought it unique. And because this time, I was doing these things in front of millions of people.

On the other side of the door stands a bellman wearing a black top hat, a long, light gray topcoat garnished with a white carnation. Underneath, a crisp white shirt, a striped tie, and charcoal pants. I take a deep breath to calm my nerves. My chin-length gray hair is smooth, my signature bob and look perfected by a stylist and a makeup artist who comes to my suite. I get a natural but flawless face, finished with a perfect red lip. Earlier that day, after an on-air interview with the BBC where I was so terrified that my agent insisted that they let me wear my sunglasses, a delivery of clothes, shoes, and bags appeared at the hotel. The logo on the garment bags says "Vivienne Westwood." I am to choose an outfit I can wear to the party my new modeling agency is throwing for me here in London to celebrate my international campaign.

On this night, like the bellman on the other side of the door, I wear a long wool topcoat. Mine is black with skinny trousers. My shirt is white, festooned with black graffiti. It secures at the neck with a pussy-bow tie. He waits for me on the other side, ready to tuck me into the waiting car. We could be mirror images. We both have gray hair. The hotel I emerge from is the preferred stay of Lady Gaga whenever she is in London. In fact, I am in the suite she usually occupies when she comes to town. It's the grandest hotel I've ever stayed in, and I'm not yet comfortable with this level of luxury, this much attention, all this fuss.

Flying over, courtesy of British Airways, I was seated in first class for the first time in my life. I felt somewhat embarrassed that I did not know what all the controls actually did and needed to ask for help. Soon after this trip, an in-flight entertainment video for this very same airline will show me confidently giving a tour of my favorite places in New York City. You would never believe it was the same woman who was sheepishly asking the flight attendant how to change my seat into a bed or who had such insecurities about really belonging in a world so unlike the one I was used to living in. I think of the saying "Fake it till you make it." While I am provided with a bed on this flight, I cannot sleep because I am so anxious about all the events my agent has planned for me. It's the invisible parts of us that are so much more complex, that contain the truth of all our human emotions and experiences. It's those parts that create distress when they are not seen.

I take the lift, as they say here, down to the lobby. I find myself in a grand entryway with towering columns and a large chandelier perfectly placed in the center of the arched ceiling. I see the revolving glass doors at the bottom of a sweeping stairway. I remember walking down the white marble steps and passing between two tall vases of exquisite blooms, changed every day. I arrive in front of the highly polished entryway, waiting for the person inside to pass through. Revolving doors seem designed for those sure about where they are going. They propel you out into the world quickly. Today, in this grand hotel, I am afraid I'll pass by the exit and keep spinning around because the person ahead of me is moving so fast. I have on boots that have never been worn. The soles and heels are slippery, causing a hesitation and carefulness rarely found in my walk.

I wait for an opening to come around. I jump in and become part of the next rotation. As I near the exit, every bone in my body wants to keep pushing on the golden brass rail, spinning around and going back inside. I look down and see the red-and-purple silk boots on my nervous feet; a brave choice for me to wear, in color and heel height. They are subtle yet transgressive. I guess these boots and choosing to wear them despite the risk they pose of falling is what this is all about. It's why people think I'm a badass.

My confidently stylish boots nudge me to hold my head a little higher and look up. As I approach the exit, my hand hesitates on the rail. I see him again, the bellhop, my mirror image, waiting. He smiles and reaches out a hand. He sees mine trembling. From his warm expression, I could imagine he recognizes me from my other life, the real one. With his smile and outstretched hand, he encourages me. I feel visible to him in a way all the other people I meet on this trip do not. I imagine he tells me to enjoy who I am becoming, to keep exploring, even if I am afraid. That what I am doing is creating some good.

I push once more, and then I'm outside. I take his white-gloved hand. It's soft and warm. He opens the door and places me gently in the car. He does not accept my tip, saying, "My pleasure." The car pulls out into the traffic and takes me through the streets of London and into the next phase of my new, very visible life. We pass a red bus that has a picture of me on its side. I touch up my bright red lips, retie my bow. I arrive. My badass boots carry me out of the car and into the crowd that waits for me. I find myself feeling a tingle of excitement about what could happen tonight—who I might meet and have a conversation with. It takes a little edge off the fear.

A few years later, when I pose another question about invisibility on Instagram, there is evidence of a more nuanced push/pull, signs that the conversation has evolved in the intervening years. I perceive, or perhaps project, a desire that one's life be witnessed. That one's life is meaningful. That we are known. For some, invisibility brings freedom: from worrying, from caring about what others may think. This anonymity helps women release an inner creativity that in earlier life was often stifled by concern about the expectations of others. More upsetting than not being noticed by potential romantic partners is a perceived lack of respect and kindness. For some women, a desire to be heard and to contribute is more important than being seen.

Some who comment feel a greater sense of control over their feeling of visibility, knowing the places where they are seen and those where they are not. They actively make choices about where they will spend their time and effort accordingly. Some women speak of moving from places with cultures of youth, where they were made to feel invisible, and proactively finding communities where how they look and where they are in life are accepted and celebrated. Women stress a desire to remain visible in both the private and public aspects of their lives, and actively seek the spaces and places where that is happening. In becoming invisible, many women have found their authentic and real selves and the freedom to explore possible selves without the regulating gaze of society.

Clear in all the responses is a longing: to be valued, to be noticed, to be given credit for the many contributions women make to their families, workplaces, communities, and society. To be visible, known, and appreciated in all of those spaces. To be viewed as the vibrant, sexual, value-added people they experience themselves to be inside. To wear whatever they damn well please. One thing is for certain: whether we are invisible or visible or both, it should always be our choice, not something that is thrust upon us by others. When I read these more recent responses, it raises the question: Is it that we wish our face and body to be visible, or is that we want to feel known?

———

The shoot is in SoHo, and the call time is 10:00 a.m. It is for a campaign in the independent magazine *Glassbook*. I buzz and wait. Someone from the magazine appears with an armful of coffees, and we enter the hallway together. At the end is a large open studio space. There are floor-to-ceiling windows, wide-plank wood floors, some antique couches, a makeup station and mirror, and three young people lounging with their coffee. A rack of clothes features metallics and sequined garments that shoot off electric currents of light. The husband-and-wife team and their assistants who will photograph me are setting up lights and screens.

There is no brief for this campaign, no preconceived idea. Unlike the shoot for the international campaign where there was a storyboard I had to fit into, this will become whatever the people in this room imagine it to be. When there is a strict schedule, when what I wear and how I wear it is determined by others, I become frozen and stiff, I suppose because someone else sees a vision they want me to conform to. I can feel their impatience when I don't quite live up to it. The rebellious part of me wants to reject it. A campaign like this, on the other hand, immediately makes me feel calm. There is the same excitement I feel when I go out to shoot with Calvin; it's a true collaboration, and you never know what can happen.

The stylist for the shoot is a small, energetic, quirky young man. The hairstylist is more of a badass than me. The makeup artist is quiet and sweet. I am offered a coffee and a seat on one of the antique couches, and we chat. During our conversation, Iris Apfel's book *Accidental Icon* comes up. It was published years after I started my blog, and many of my older followers took umbrage at this. I am not upset; after all, I do not own the copyright or trademark to the name. When the topic comes up during our coffee chat, the team decides that the best approach is to change my name rather than raise a fuss. They come up with "Accidentally Iconic," proclaiming it a more active voice and a better fit for who they think I am. This begins a wildly fun and imaginative conversation about creating that persona.

They ask about my favorite time of life, what I was doing when I was happiest and how I experienced myself inside. Garments are pulled, shoes gathered, jewelry selected, hair and makeup done with each look. One features a fierce red cat eye, a gold slip dress, a sheer black top with sparkles, knee socks with crystal flowers and pink suede slide heels. Each member of the team's opinion is taken seriously, and there is a respect from the creative director and the photographers for who they are as creatives and artists. Everyone is seen. I'm a full-fledged member of the team. Transported back in time, I am preparing to go disco dancing. Dancing was my life in the 1970s. I lived for the weekends, which could sometimes start as early as Thursday night. It was the time I wore makeup, messed up my hair, wore clothes I never wore in my very serious and responsible job. Society had written roles and scripts for me as a woman of twenty-five, and they were always a burden. While dancing I let them all go. I could live in a world where anything was possible, where I could decide who I wanted to be.

The photos that come from this *Glassbook* shoot are my favorite photos out of all the independent magazine features I appeared in that year. This team of exceptionally talented young people recognized and represented the woman I am inside. They chose not to make me a stereotype. They did not tell me to stay in my lane. They really wanted to show me, to reveal my complexity. In doing so, they cared about and for me. They met, spoke to, and collaborated with the woman inside—the sexual woman, the woman who loves life, who remains the rebel, the disco queen, the provocateur, yet is vulnerable too. When the photographers sent me the photos, I felt overwhelming joy and happiness. When my sister saw them, she said, "That's exactly how you looked when you were twenty-five, yet somehow you are still the age you are."

So many times, a comment like this appears on my feed: "I am 25 going on 26, and as I age, I am terrified to get older." How very terrible is it that one fears the end before life has even really begun? That women are only important, beautiful, and "seen" for a brief period of their lives, in an era when we are expected to live until eighty and beyond? When I ask younger women about their fears about invisibility, they tell me, "I want to keep feeling like myself and not have that self disappear when I am old." The self they are referring to is our idealized twenty-five-year-old self. I try to remind them that youth is not a stand-in for a self. I want women to know that while our bodies may change, the self is ours to imagine; it never leaves us. When we are old, there is often a disconnect between our chronological age and how old we feel on the inside. Some days I feel like I am twenty-one; others, I may feel like I am fifty. When I am feeling and experiencing life as my eighteen-year-old self and others respond to me as if I am old, I experience a jarring dissonance. It happens at times when I look in the mirror, and the older version of me looks back. All the ages we have ever been live inside us. They can be accessible to us as creative muses. They are not visible unless people choose to see them and we choose to express them, as I did this day with this team of coconspirators. They saw the me inside, the me on the outside, the me that was me on that day. All invited to the party, and all invited to dance.

When I look at the photos taken during the *Glassbook* shoot, not only do I feel seen, I feel known. It was after this fashion shoot that I finally made the connection. All the emails, comments, and thank-yous I'd received finally clicked for me. I humbly admit, I did not always understand the level of gratitude. I do now. That in me being seen, people feel they are being seen, or at least feel entitled to be seen. They feel recognized, and that makes them remember the woman inside. It gives them the courage to let her come out: the woman who loves fashion, sees herself in a mohawk, and has been told she is too old for it; the woman who dreamed of being a painter but thought she had lost that chance after a life taken over by work and parenting. Young people who receive scary, awful messages about getting older see that they do not have to disappear or face a life of loneliness and despair simply by doing something we all do from the moment we are born: get older.

Standards of youth and beauty create harm not just to those who are not visible but also to those who are already being threatened by this terrible fear of disappearing if you do not meet those standards. Stereotypes about who we are that are not reflective of who we really are take their toll not only on our spirit but on our body and physical health too. Promoting negative stereotypes that result in negative thoughts about being old or getting old, regardless of what age we are, affects our physical, mental, and cognitive health, making us more prone to illness and a shorter life-span as we age. Will there ever come a time when we transcend the societal constructions of our bodies? As a start, perhaps we need to ask ourselves the question "Who do you really want to be visible to, and why?" Somehow I get the sense that as I continue my journey as Accidental Icon, this will be an important question for me to answer.

65

Don't Be Influenced (Even If You're an Influencer)

There are certain periods in life when the desire for independence becomes a singular pursuit. It happens during toddlerhood, adolescence, midlife, and older age. Accidental Icon behaves much like my two-year-old granddaughter. We run headlong into adventures. We test limits and push boundaries. We take risks, some leading to success, some to failure, and have a tantrum or two along the way. We are delighted with each new discovery. We sleep like a rock every night because we spend our days running from one new thing to the next. Our brains are laying down new pathways. We are always ready to head someplace new.

For various reasons having to do with her job, my daughter adamantly demands that her image and name not appear on any of my platforms. My daughter is far more beautiful than I. She refuses to accept any mother/daughter opportunities, even when they could be quite lucrative for us both. When she was nine, when I anxiously responded to her distress with solution after solution, she would look me in the eye and say, "Just shut up and hold me!" The one thing I can always depend on is that she will always tell me like it is. She will never say yes when she doesn't mean it just to please someone else, including me. This tells you something about her personality. There are so many things I love about her, but that characteristic is what I love most, even during the times it may hurt me.

One mother/daughter opportunity comes along where

we negotiate a concession of sorts. While my daughter will not appear, she agrees to let my two-year-old granddaughter take part. The shoot is part of my salvaged relationship with Refinery29, so I am happy about this. My son-in-law drives in from the suburbs, and we meet in a bagel shop close to the studio we will shoot in. As usual, my granddaughter is wildly excited to see me and runs all around the café. I was present at the moment of her birth, and we've been close ever since. Despite the best intentions of her dad, she refuses to be corralled. I wonder if she will ever hold still long enough for the photographer to get a photo.

We arrive at the studio, and she immediately captivates everyone on the set. She has hazel eyes like her mom, as well as her very direct gaze. Both mother and daughter have mastered a certain look, that leaves the recipient to wonder, "What the hell have I done now?" My granddaughter has brown hair with blond highlights, cut short. Her lips are pouty and pink. The stylist has a clothing rack that includes looks for us both. I get my granddaughter to sit still in my lap by letting her look in my purse and take everything out. Whenever we are together, getting into my bag is an irresistible pursuit of forbidden fruit, even though I swiftly remove it and tell her no. The stylist shows the outfit chosen for me: a long white shirtdress with detachable black leather sleeves fastened under my neck with a buckle. Well, this woman gets me. I approve.

It's a different story when she brings out her selections for my granddaughter. Still on my lap as I try to place adorable dresses over her head, the toddler screams, "No!" When I attempt to force the issue, a tantrum ensues. My son-in-law apologizes to the crew.

This episode reminds me of my daughter's unshakable refusal to wear any shirt or dress that has a button. She can't explain it herself, and I've never understood why she finds an innocent button so offensive. This did not conform to the idealized Gap kid's prep look I envisioned for her in her childhood, and after several tantrums I had to give in and return the clothes. Perhaps her resistance to buttons is related to her propensity to steadfastly refuse to take on any projections about who she is that her father or I might have unconsciously tried to impose. He and I were both preppy at the time. She is decidedly not. To this day, when I try to pass along an expensive designer look, if it has an opening secured with a button, I'm greeted with a polite but firm "Thank you. But no." I think it's not about disliking buttons per se but her way of continuing to say, "I'm not you, Mom."

I stand up and hold my granddaughter in my arms to calm her. We walk over to the rack. Hanging there in all their tantalizing glory are a pair of sparkly gold pants. Her hand reaches out to grab them, and the stylist and I laugh. This time, when I pull them on, there are no tears. Wearing a cream-colored embroidered peasant blouse with the pants, she looks serious but adorable in the photo that is finally selected. She seems to have a look on her face that says, "Don't mess with me. I know what I want." While I still wear my sunglasses, my large hoop earrings are absent, tucked away from the little hands that would surely want to pull them off my ears. Neither of us is smiling. Probably because there is someone in the background telling us to.

Yves Saint Laurent once said, "Fashions fade, style is eternal." What I admire about this quote and the designer who said it is that Saint Laurent is challenging the very system that made him famous. He is saying that style is situated within a single person and transcends time because it's so personal. Style is unique and individual. Fashion is a body dressed by others. The "dressed by others" part, for someone like me and the women in my family, is like throwing down some kind of gauntlet. My mother and grandmother before me, my daughter and granddaughter after me, and I myself all push against the status quo by being the one in control of what we will or will not wear. Our bodies and our decisions about what we put on them belong to us. We retain the right of first refusal.

As my granddaughter and daughter do with what others want them to wear, we refuse. My mother and grandmother do. I do. We are stubbornly independent. People unfortunately confuse assertiveness with aggression and anger when it comes to girls and women; when we defend ourselves, hold strong opinions, and are verbally self-assured, they consider us confrontational or rude. Most likely for that reason, at various times, others refer to the women who share my DNA as "belligerent." While the term *intergenerational belligerence* refers to conflict between generations, to me it signifies a kind of independence of thought and action passed from one generation of women in my family to the next.

Four years into the Accidental Icon journey, in 2018, I found myself working with people—agents, editors, art directors, brands, photographers, stylists—who had their own ideas about who I should be, what I should do, and what direction I should take this new career in. They thought I should shoot in color and wear clothes that were not only black and white, clothes I might not wear in my everyday life. They had more experience, they would say, and knew the rules of this game better than I, a neophyte who, for heaven's sake, came from the field of social welfare. I guess they conveniently forgot that it was this clueless newbie who had got herself featured in media all over the world, garnered more than half a million followers on Instagram, and was the person with whom it was now in their best interest to work.

I have always suspected people of trying to take away my independence because, as a girl and a woman, I have always found myself in contexts where that is in fact the case. In fairness, my agents—I've worked now with four of them—also remember the clueless woman who didn't read the fine print and was sometimes naive. They have been here to protect me. They have been here to help me make enough of an income to retire from academia and live a less stressful and more creative life. A part of me knows all of this, and remains eternally grateful to them all. Yet when I feel like any of these people are telling me what to do or what to wear, my natural instinct is to rebel. Even when it may not be in my best interest to do so.

I learned how to maintain dignity and self-respect, even in the face of humiliation, from my grandmother. My mother's mother was widowed suddenly at the same age I was when I started Accidental Icon. She sold everything she owned, including her home in Connecticut, and moved to Dallas to live with her two sisters, all three widowed during the same year. As young women, the sisters performed as a trio; one sister played the harp, one the piano, and my grandmother the cello. They traveled often, and that is what they did for the next twenty years—this time without their instruments and husbands.

We saw my grandmother during this period maybe four times a year. She would call and tell us to meet her at the New York piers or the airport, when she and her sisters were embarking on a European adventure or a trip to Asia. My grandmother, in an exquisitely tailored bouclé suit, would envelop us in a cloud of expensive perfume. The jingle of the charm bracelets she wore on her slender wrist announced her arrival. She would bring gifts—pearls from Japan, or perfume from Paris—upon her return. For me there were geisha dolls, books of watercolor scenes of cherry blossoms on rice paper with transparent covers, carved perfume bottles, and netsukes made of wood.

Sometimes she would stay for more than a flyby, and there

would be a shopping trip to the city for a new outfit for me. I remember one time in particular when she took me shopping for a special Easter outfit and chose a pair of shoes to go along with it. Constructed of the softest white kidskin, they were as graceful as ballet slippers. In fact, Capezio made them. The final achingly exquisite touch was a pearl button that fastened the strap. We both just sighed in appreciation as we looked at the shoe on my outstretched foot. After shopping, we shared tea and chocolate eclairs at Charleston Gardens, the café at the old B. Altman on Fifth Avenue. Both voracious readers, we would trade stories from the books we were reading, and she would tell me about her travels.

When I was younger, I believed my grandmother to be the most glamorous woman I knew. My mother was so angry with her. I could not understand why. The women who were constants in my daily life were housewives—often unhappy, apron strings tying them to their homes as they conformed to the role of 1950s housewives—and nuns, with vows of poverty, chastity, and, most alarming, obedience. In comparison, my grandmother was an exciting and inspirational figure who offered me a glimpse of what life could be for a woman freed from masculine or societal authority. I admire my grandmother for being such a rebel, doing something most women of her time did not dare to do. I think, however, that as her money ran out at the end and she rotated miserably between her resentful daughters' homes—I remember my mother and her sisters arguing about who should have her next—she may have had some regrets. Yet even when completely dependent on the goodwill and financial support of her daughters and their spouses, she always maintained her dignity. She accomplished this through how she chose to dress. And yes, there were times when she did not do what her daughters wanted her to. I remember hearing them talk among themselves about how belligerent she was.

My grandmother's daily ritual of dressing fascinated me. She slept with a satin cap to keep her coiffed hair intact until her next weekly salon appointment. She always wore a negligee to bed, with matching satin slippers. She removed the lace-paneled robe and laid it across the foot of her bed. She drank tea, not coffee, in the morning. First, she applied the lotions and skin care products that stayed packed in a camel-colored hardshell makeup case she kept by her bed, even though she no longer traveled. Next would be the powder, then lipstick on the cheeks and on her lips. She'd spritz her perfume on the inside of her slim wrists. Then she would laboriously pull on a waist-to-knee girdle and lift her pendulous breasts into a bra. Next would be a half slip followed by a dress, or some days a skirt and a blouse. In direct opposition to my granddaughter's preference, I never saw her wear pants. At last she would add her collection of bracelets to her left wrist and, for the finishing touch, slip into a pair of low kid-skin heels. All this dressing ritual for a woman who now had nothing to do but sit in a chair in our living room and read or knit. Yet there was something so very admirable in her determination to maintain the routines from a life she no longer had. The way she dressed each day showed her great desire to keep her dignity and bodily autonomy, and it lasted until the day she died.

I'm excited. I'm going to be featured in a video for an international edition of *Vogue*. The set is in Williamsburg, Brooklyn. I take the J train to the address on my call sheet, a decrepit row house under the subway. It gives me pause; something about this just doesn't feel right, but when I buzz and am let in by a production assistant, I see that the set is actually a nicely furnished apartment. I am the only talent listed on the call sheet, so I wonder what kind of story this is going to be. All I am told is that it will make use of the concept of what a badass I am when it comes to age. I'm introduced to the director, the videographer, the stylist, and the hair and makeup persons. There is a rack with clothes, a table with makeup, hair products, and styling tools. The island in front of the kitchen area holds fruit, nuts, candy, water, and coffee.

The director is close to my age, and from the moment I walk in, she makes it clear that she is in charge. She's the tallest person in the room, with shoulder-length black hair, a sharp nose, and a downturned mouth. When her assistant shows me the storyboard, it's full of clichés about age like "60 is the new 40." The director wears a short skirt, a transparent cream-colored V-neck blouse, and high black heels. My grandmother would call the look on her face "sour," and subsequently add how unattractive it was. I am a good eight inches shorter than her, and dressed comfortably in jeans, a white shirt, black Yohji blazer, and black leather flats. I introduce myself. She nods; I am dismissed. No small talk from her. She issues orders a mile a minute, and the crew runs around, trying to please her. She does not like where a pillow is placed, the way the furniture is arranged. They scurry to fix it. My initial impression is that the entire scene is a little tacky, but hey, this is *Vogue*. Let's see what happens.

After the set is prepared to her liking, she walks to the rack and with one hand pulls out a black leather miniskirt and a short biker jacket with studs. Her other hand picks up a pair of thigh-high black leather boots. She walks up to me and says, "You can use the bathroom to change. This is what you are wearing." Her arms stretch out to hand me the clothes. I do not extend mine. If I ever put on that hideous outfit, I'm thinking, I'll look like a caricature of an old lady trying to look young. I'm a badass in part because I'm an older woman who is decidedly not trying to look young.

In the silence that ensues after I fail to reach out for the clothes in her arms, I can sense all the crew in the room holding their breath. Everyone is waiting to see what I will do. I finally say firmly, "I'm not wearing that."

It takes every ounce of my self-control not to laugh out loud at the look on her face. *No* is clearly not a word she often hears. I observe the horrified looks on the faces of the crew. To them, saying no could mean never being hired again in the small world of New York fashion. I suppose this is a real benefit of being old: I have learned that saying no to some things actually makes me more desirable.

"What do you mean you're not wearing it?" she says. "It will look really cool. I'd wear it in a heartbeat."

"I'm not wearing it," I say, "and it will look exactly the opposite of cool." Unspoken are the words *I am not you.* Even when I'm taking risks with my fashion choices, particularly in projects for independent magazines, I always make sure I look dignified. I will not allow this woman to trespass on that.

After more back-and-forth, seeing I will not budge, she gives an exasperated sigh, turns to the stylist and says, "Find her something else to wear." She stalks off to make a call on her phone, probably to my agent to complain about my belligerence. The crew's exhaled breath fills the room with a new and better kind of energy.

The stylist pulls out a garment bag she had not hung on the rack. Inside is the most delicious assortment of clothes. Every look is something I would wear. Some are things I am deliriously excited to wear. She confides that she follows me on Instagram and knew I would never wear what the director wanted me to, so she pulled some alternatives. I end up wearing Miu Miu. I emerge from the bathroom in a soft terra-cotta knit bra and shorts, covered by a transparent print shirtdress. Tulle knee socks and platforms. A long coat with a wide, pointed orange collar and an orange flower print on black wool. There are layers of complexity in the many garments that make up this look. I can reveal or conceal, but that decision is mine to make. Empowered in these clothes, I resist the clichés in the script by doing a little rewriting of my own. The director thinks I am a belligerent pain in the ass. I am.

The stylist who chose these garments in her own way said no too. Thinking independently, she brought her secret stash of clothes. I am grateful she conveyed her knowledge and respect of who I am. I'm happy that I value myself enough to say no. Because of the stylist and what I ended up wearing, we created the conditions for dignity to enter the set that had been absent before. On the J train home, I wear a self-satisfied smile. Sort of like the one my grandmother wore when she emerged from her room in full makeup and dressed to the nines, even though she had no place to go.

After a long run with my undercut bob, toward the end of my sixty-fifth year I feel in need of something new. I cut my hair very short, like a boy. My agent asks, "Why did you cut your hair?" I sense some disapproval. My new haircut, I think on an unconscious level, is my response to the times we are living in. The #MeToo movement is picking up steam, fueled by prominent women sharing their stories and social media's ability to make a cause or an issue go viral. I can still feel the power of the Women's March last year. I'm hanging on to the pink pussy hat that sits on the top shelf of my closet. A designer friend has made me one in black. I sense a fight brewing. There seems to be a need for women to feel their own power. For me that means an androgynous and punky look. I am taken by the Dior campaigns this year, where women wear short hair, leather berets, and clothes that are utilitarian yet feminine because of their cut. T-shirts say "We Should All Be Feminists." There are men's caps with netted veils. The model Ruth Bell serves as my current haircut inspiration. Every time I cut my hair very short, I think of my mother. Somehow, cutting my hair short feels like a transgression. Most times it is not immediately clear why I feel a need to rebel or misbehave; I just feel it coming.

My mother has always expressed her rebellious nature covertly, seeming more conforming on the surface, but not really. The rest of us evidence more overt behaviors, accompanied by loud verbal pronouncements. My mother shows rather than tells. My mother is the parent who named me. On my birth certificate appears the masculine form of my name, Lyn (not the feminine Lynn), and Marie attached with a hyphen. When questioned about its origin, she gives the vague and unsatisfactory answer that it's the name of some child she used to babysit. She's often inscrutable. I examine old photographs and observe that my mother always cut my hair short like a boy, yet I wear pastel-colored frilly dresses and never pants or shorts. Her big concession to shorts seems to be a sun suit with an elaborate ruffled butt. There's one photo, though, that stands out for me. It's black and white, and in it I'm four. I'm dressed in an oversize black suit and a bowler hat, a bit too big for my head. Towering above me, wearing a deep scowl, a long, white dress, and a shimmery veil, is my friend Donald. On the photo's edge is my mother, grinning like the Cheshire Cat, with a very short haircut.

Somehow, as I look back at these photos today, I can't help but think my name came more from the discontent with strict gender roles simmering beneath the surface of compliance during the 1950s than from a child my mother used to babysit. In her playful rejection of strict gender roles for me, she opened the door to the idea that how you decide to cut your hair or what you decide to wear can be a way to refuse. In her case, it was what you decide not to wear.

For my grandmother, getting dressed expressed her desire to be treated with dignity and keep a sense of autonomy. In her later life, my mother no longer wants to get dressed at all. As my mother's dementia progresses, she performs a kind of parallel strip tease; as each level of functioning fades, she sheds a new piece of her clothing, until in the last months of her life, she insists on being completely naked.

It started when she was the age I am now, and refused to wear a bra. My sister and I engaged in wrestling matches with her powerful will, imploring her to put it on when we were taking her out. We bought every kind of bra imaginable, hoping there would be one comfortable enough for her to wear. We often found them tossed in the garbage. This throwing away of bras is a protest, like that of her peers in the 1960s, while she was stuck at home in suburbia. She was heavily endowed. I, less so. I didn't really need a bra until I was sixteen. As I write this now, at age sixty-nine, I'm not wearing one. Now I get it, though I admit I put one on when I leave the house. And yes, like my grandmother, I have to give my boobs a little help in getting settled inside.

After the bra came the shirt. We walked into her room and

found her topless. She said it was because they kept the heat too high for the benefit of those "old people" who lived with her, and she was hot. Next were the shoes and socks, finally the pants. For a time we joined with the staff in believing that in order to keep her dignity, she needed to be dressed. As things progressed, we understood what this rebellion meant to her and supported her in it. After a life of constraints imposed by religion, family, and society, she wanted to be free at the end. We received phone calls or were called into meetings to address our mother's "belligerent" refusal to get dressed. When aides tried to force her, she threw tantrums like a child. At the end of her life, much of our advocacy efforts were related to how she could remain naked in a respectful and dignified way.

─────────────

My grandmother made clear her deep disappointment with my mother's choice to "abandon her class" through her choice of a partner who didn't finish high school, much less graduate from college. She swapped the latest styles from Saks or B. Altman for E. J. Korvette. In an achingly beautiful gesture, each Christmas my father, who must have squirreled away money all year, would gift my mother one very expensive outfit from Brooks Brothers, an acknowledgement of her sacrifice and of his love. My father had what we call "a good eye," and when she donned these clothes, my mother suddenly appeared beautiful and glamorous, someone different from the mother we knew.

I remember now my favorite of these outfits, a skirt and

matching cardigan in a shade that whispered the color yellow. It was of the softest, most luxurious cashmere. The cardigan had small, flat, circular pearl buttons. The sensual feel of the garment was such a contrast to the scratchy, abrasive texture of the usual polyester clothes that came from the discount store. You could rest in these garments, sleep in them. It was one of the very few articles of clothing my mother owned that seemed worthy of the perfect strand of pearls my grandmother had brought her from Japan, making sure that we knew she had observed the divers, mainly women, as they dove deep into the cold to gather treasure from the bottom of the sea. That it was one outfit, one time a year, and gifted with love and gratitude, made it infinitely more special in how my mother wore and animated it and how others perceived it. She would remark that just one well-made, high-quality outfit a year was more than enough, her version of treasure. Perhaps this is what made it so easy for her to shed all her clothes at the end of her life; she had never had a lot of them.

As I scroll back in time to retrieve photos on my phone to help me remember as I write this book, it startles me to see photo after photo of my mother in the throes of her decline. These are images of my mother during her last days on earth. I don't have an awareness of taking these photos. Perhaps it is the same unconscious impulse that prompted me to start Accidental Icon when I turned sixty-one: the middle finger up to the dictate that you must become invisible. The fear that you will stop being seen as beautiful. In all the photos, my mother is asleep, either in bed or in the reclining chair we got her, and in various stages of undress. In some pictures she pulls the sheet up high, revealing the cross of her graceful legs, tapering into the slim ankles I always envied. I flash back to an old black-and-white photo of her in a beach chair, age twenty-six. The look on her face and the pose of her legs are the same.

In other photos I took during this time of her decline, it is her peaceful expression or the light from the window reflecting on her smooth cheek. Her skin is transparent and luminous. There are images that reveal the elegant, sensual curve of her shoulder peeking out from under a sheet, as if it were a strapless gown. It is seductive. In the beach photo, she wears a one-piece bathing suit. She has lowered the straps, in effect making it strapless, as she always preferred an even tan. While you can't see the color of the suit in this old photo, my mind's eye recalls it as red.

As I look at these recent photos, I see a sensuality that one would never expect to see during such frailty, from a body breaking down organ by organ. I see her saying no, in the way she says no, showing, not telling. Her "No" is full of beauty, grace, and dignity. Each generation contributes their unique way of saying no that forms a strand, not of pearls, like the ones my grandmother brought us, but of our DNA. Intergenerational belligerence, passed down like an heirloom piece of jewelry from generation to generation of women. I did not know how close I would need to keep it, as I continued on this journey of being the Accidental Icon.

66

Always Balance
Risk and Reward

I am sixty-six when I take my first trip to Paris. I can't believe my luck and privilege that this first trip is all-expenses-paid, and during the city's Fashion Week. I'm here at the invitation of Maison Martin Margiela to celebrate—or let's be transparent, to promote—a new perfume. I also get to attend Margiela's runway show. My badass reputation is a good fit, or so the PR agency sees it, with the name of the scent: Mutiny. The press release announces, "The juice and its flacon reflect the deconstruction and subversion epitomized by the house and transform the techniques of Maison Margiela into the defiant character of Mutiny." My caption on the sponsored post I produce says, "Deconstructing and reconstructing what it means to be older, that's my Mutiny."

This is my first real-life visit to Paris, one that is not a daydream fueled by novels and beautiful editorials. Staying in a hotel right next door to the original Chanel store (with Coco Chanel's apartment upstairs), I am footsteps away from rue Saint-Honoré. I steal a moment to wander this street, with its many boutiques and perfume shops. I buy myself a different bottle of perfume, not the one I am promoting. Its name is Another 13. It is a gender-neutral scent that mimics the scent of paper, and is meant for those who like to write. Mentioning Colette as a muse, the trained lab technician follows a protocol of strict instructions to create Another 13. As she hands me my bottle, marked "Paris" with today's date, the salesperson tells me this scent is actually a collaboration between the perfumery and Jefferson Hack, the editor of my favorite fashion magazines: *Dazed* and *Another Magazine*. The reviews suggest it smells just like a newly opened, freshly printed magazine. I spritz some on my wrist, bring it to my nose.

Because of the need to sandwich travel in between the days I teach, I'm here in Paris for about forty-eight hours. During this brief time I fit in breakfast with the founder of a brand that I now often wear in my photos and lunch with the woman from Vancouver who has become my eyewear stylist, get filmed for a promotional video, attend a runway show, visit the Acne Studios showroom to try on and pull clothes, and attend a celebratory dinner and a late-night event in a warehouse on the outskirts of Paris.

Margiela and Dazed Beauty cosponsored the late-night event, a rave of sorts. I am elated to find Jefferson Hack in attendance. I am beside myself, meeting him, because I have budding literary aspirations. The most exciting thing that happened this year is that I signed with a literary agent. I have hopes, as does she, for a book. I have dreams of a life that is shaped more around writing. My own online magazine? Maybe a column in an independent magazine? I write about these ambitions on my blog.

The venue has a monochromatic color scheme, bespoke projections, a #MyMutiny Airstream bus, and flyer-posted walls. In the photo of me that appears in Getty Images, I stand in front of the wall, light bouncing off my face and the gold satin skirt of the dress I wear. An oversize Acne Studios blazer completes my look. I have a very smoky eye, hair and makeup courtesy of the team that got me ready earlier in the day for the video. I actually know some people there, proof of my building network in the industry. As always, there are also people who know me from the internet, even though I don't know them. Thanks to Instagram, people soon find out I am in Paris.

As word gets out that I'm here, a host of invitations find their way to me via DM. They are to the shows of my beloved brands like Yohji Yamamoto, Issey Miyake, and Comme des Garçons. There are events that precede and follow the shows. It's excruciatingly painful, but I must decline them all. I have to return to New York to teach my Thursday class and must say no to invitations I've worked for four years to receive. This is one no it does not feel good to say. Losing these opportunities hits me hard. I can no longer put off the reality that if I want to see Accidental Icon continue to grow, have time to write, and accept the exciting opportunities to travel that are coming my way, I can no longer hold a full-time academic position.

In the fall of 2018, when I return from my trip to Paris, I call my dean's secretary and ask if she has any open time on her calendar. My office and the dean's are at the Lincoln Center campus, a block away from where the early adventures of Accidental Icon first took place. She and I are mutual fans. We think alike when it comes to technology and the way the world is shifting because of it, and she has supported my Accidental Icon journey. We sit at her round table, and I think she knows what I'm about to say. She does not want to see me go but always knew this day would come. I intend to retire. I hand her the official letter.

Because I am "retiring," I think about risk. I think about leaving a societally sanctioned, predictable, low-risk environment to enter a space that is yet undefined. I think about economics and what is going on in the world now and perhaps in the immediate future. I must admit that what began as a creative project and vehicle to express myself has now grown into a plausible way to make a living, but not always in a predictable way. The unpredictability scares me. I worry about making a sustainable income. If I need to get another job, my age is not in my favor. I share on my blog my struggles with not losing myself, being ethical about all of it, and remaining true to my purpose. The possibility that I may lose the battle worries me. I know myself and know how anxious not having enough money makes me. I've excavated my history and understand that childhood experiences of living with less, the consequences of my parents never having enough money, and the anxiety (and humiliation) I witnessed and experienced around that fact have resulted in a worrisome scarcity approach even when it's clear I have enough.

When I think of my project of creating Accidental Icon, most of the time it brings me pleasure. I get a deeply satisfying feeling when I am creating and communicating, whether

I am writing, envisioning content, or meeting others who know more about this space than I do or share with me a commitment to always learning. This state of satisfaction, like other stimulants of pleasure, makes me want to do it more and all the time. The architect of the pleasure experience is the reward system laid down in our brain. What rewards will I grant myself now? Moving to a position of doing this full-time means I must determine a manageable equation between risk and reward. Looking back now, perhaps these anxieties caused a miscalculation. The question I will soon confront because of this decision is: What kind of reward is most valuable?

But the taste I got of irresistible adventures on my trip to Paris, with the promise of more to come, is much more seductive than any of my concerns. The following year, there will be another trip to Paris. I get to stay an entire week. Once again, while there, I have an experience that will change the trajectory of my life. The next time I will be wiser than I am now.

Once I am no longer teaching, I have the time and the inclination to attend more of the events I'm invited to. When asked, "What do you do?" I always begin by saying, "Until this past September I was a professor, but now, um, er, I guess maybe I'm a . . . ," and then get tongue-tied. I begin a long, meandering explanation of how I came to be in this room to create content to post on Instagram. I appear confused about what I do, and consequently about who I am. I soon learn that I'm what's known as a social media influencer, but when people ask, I hesitate to own this aspect of my identity. Unlike social work or being a professor, I have not chosen it. It's something that was given to me without my permission. I don't like the sound of it—a red flag I ignore.

This form of work is contemporary, having become an official occupation around 2016. The word *influencer* first appeared in the dictionary this year, 2019. It has two definitions. The first, "A person who inspires or guides the actions of others," is an apt description of who I am and what I was doing as the Accidental Icon in the years that led up to this one. I've inspired many women to feel and think differently about what it means to be older. I am someone who keeps serving up the potential of this time of life. Who appears rebellious and free. A person known as authentic and real. An ordinary woman who has crafted an interesting life. I encourage others to do the same. My blog, mostly, contains these parts of the definition.

On my blog, I write about my struggles, dreams, fashion, and the state of what I call What Nowness. We have an unlimited number of opportunities to reinvent ourselves. I am authentic in that I share when I am tired and uninspired. When my house is a mess, or I am. When I am stressed and eat too much ice cream. When I'm behind on doctor's appointments. When I miss my weekly visit with my mother, and how bad that makes me feel. I apologize for not blogging consistently, suddenly missing weeks at a time thanks to the busyness of Accidental Icon's schedule. I reveal how I sit on the couch in front of my suitcase, having to unpack and pack it again and cry to Calvin. I do not want to leave him and go on another trip. I write about how much I want to have time to write, and of course, the aspiration of editing an online magazine. I write stories where clothes are objects that help us think about something else, something greater. Looking back, it's quite interesting to see what I do not write about. I never write about how I am actually making my income. I write about how I wish I was making my income.

Everything else appears on my Instagram page. The other definition of an influencer is someone who companies pay to show and describe their products on social media, encouraging others to buy them. If you look at my Instagram feed during 2019, you'll see a woman riding e-bikes, using a credit card all over the city, sleeping in new linens, wearing sneakers she has no time to run in, and using beauty products that cost more money per month to use than she pays for her monthly rent. She creates online shopping platforms and store gift guides for the holidays. Her bags and coats cost thousands, lent for a photo while consignment store clothes fill her closet. She appears to drink wine when she doesn't drink at all. There are shoes she will never wear more than once. There are posts that reveal she's in commercials for drugstores and websites too. She travels to Madrid to promote a hotel, Tokyo a shirt, Paris a perfume, California to suggest supplements, and back again to show a new wide screen for video calls. Only one trip is a real fashion campaign. For that one, she travels to Iceland. She appears at fashion weeks, the stock exchange, expensive restaurants, hotels, cruise ships, and department stores. She wears magenta polka-dot dresses she would never otherwise put on and makes funny videos meant to sell a purse.

The paid partnership banners unfurl over more and more of her posts. The commercial photographer she hires takes most of these photos. She has to ensure that the products get photographed according to the brief. Calvin's lack of proficiency with Photoshop no longer serves Accidental Icon. In between sponsored posts I throw up photos that Calvin has taken, in which I wear my own clothes, in my everyday ordinary life. I take "staycations." I travel through boroughs, not continents. While the other photos make her a lot of money, these are the ones that get many thousands more likes.

———————————————

I think the moment I began to lose control of it all was when I reluctantly agreed to let someone else design me a new website. I love my website. I built it myself on Squarespace in the first days of Accidental Icon, and I'm proud of it. It is my center. My heart. All the arteries and veins that are now part of Accidental Icon lead back to it. Because I built it, I know it, and know how to do everything I want or need to do on it. I designed it for writing a short essay and posting the photo that inspires it. I spent days picking out just the right font. I can confidently say, "That's my platform."

But the brand we are negotiating doing a commercial and multiyear contract with hosts websites and wants to design me a new one as part of the campaign. I resist for a time. My poor patient agent has to put up with me whining and crying about it for months. I dislike every version the design team hired by the brand sends me. Thanks to the negotiation skills of my agent, in the final rendition there is some slight resemblance to the minimal aesthetic of my original site.

No matter how many tutorials I receive or consultants the brand hires to help me, I can never learn to do more than post a photo and write an essay on my shiny new website. My body resists, my mind refuses to remember. I just can't own it. I can't understand how it works. It never feels like "my platform." Because it isn't. The name of the campaign is "Make the World You Want." To be honest, at first I was excited to make this commercial because I really liked the concept. Set among fantastical scenes created in a massive studio in LA, it showed a young girl searching for what she wanted to do with her life. In the commercial she wanders through sets that represent the websites of myself and three other creatives who have designed independent new careers for themselves, of which these websites are an important component. "Make the World You Want" was a statement of empowerment, one I endorsed. My set was a runway that had arches of brilliant light. I stomped down it in full badassery mode, although the glass floor, lit from below, was quite slippery.

This commercial was probably the most celebrated and hated performance I engaged in as Accidental Icon. The commercial included me speaking the words "Age is just an illusion." It ran on every cable channel and was played over and over. While I was fairly well known on both US coasts, in Europe, and in China and Japan, this was my first introduction to everyday America. I heard and saw myself say those words in airports, in restaurants, and on TV in North Dakota, St. Louis, and Atlanta. It was all over Facebook and YouTube.

Prior to this commercial, I had the good fortune of having overall positive comments and responses, with very few haters or trolls. While many women applauded my bright red suit and arrogant moxie in the commercial, there were comments and DMs from women who were furious with me for so narcissistically and casually tossing out the idea that aging was not real, because for them it was. Some were widows, had lost friends in middle age, been discriminated against at work, had to work well into their older age, been burdened with caretaking responsibilities while also suffering poor health from years of chronic poverty, lack of affordable health care, or simply because of where they lived or what group they belonged to. But all were dealing with very real aspects and consequences of aging. How brave and wonderful of them to call me out. They were trying to tell me that an active, comfortable, and long old age is a privilege not equally shared.

My initial response to those I perceived as "trolls" was to ignore them, but this time something made me listen and engage. In a conversation with one woman, I understood the harm that came from saying aging was not real. How I was erasing the experience of thousands, probably millions, of women. I'm not putting myself down here. I take a certain amount of pride that I moved the needle a bit for some older and younger women. I gave some of them courage to resist stereotypes or scripts others were writing for them—to do and wear whatever the hell they wanted. Yet I also take pride in my commitment to being a critical thinker, and that means taking a very hard look at one's own self in a continuous process. I very much believe in hope and am happy to have provided it to some, but I now know that the hope I was providing was not inclusive.

In my conversation with this woman, I acknowledged that saying those words was a bad choice. I should have been more thoughtful. I was sorry. There are many women without the resources to "Make the World You Want" (as the commercial proclaims) when they are old. The woman I spoke with accepted my apology by saying maybe I wasn't the arrogant asshole she originally thought me to be because I had taken the time to engage with her and not write her off as a troll. I wish I could say that I significantly changed what I was doing after that, but I can't because it took me until the pandemic to stop long enough to think again in a critically reflective way. As a social worker and professor, I had always been deeply aware of my privilege. Critical reflection was a part of my practice; as a social media influencer in a world that moves at scrolling speed, it pulled me into an undertow of self-importance with no time to think. At some point, I stopped being a unique person and became a brand. I forgot I had a body. I colluded in my own disappearing by becoming an "influencer" in the capitalist sense of the word, not an influencer of culture change as I had originally started out to be.

I must take ownership, I'm not a victim, I agreed to it all. I confess I was in awe of the creativity exhibited in the sets and enjoyed the experience of filming a commercial. I'm a "performer," after all. But this is what made it all so hard. There were parts of what I was doing that I loved and parts that I hated. Ambivalence creates a netherland where there are conflicting desires of equal strength. It puts you into a state of indecisiveness. It makes you feel stuck. For me, it took from my creativity and passion.

I'm not placing blame. I take full responsibility for the fact that I began to lose myself and found some of my values slipping away. I now understand why. It was easy for me to take risks and leap into the unknown when I had the secure base of a full-time academic job, with all its benefits to jump from. Maybe I'm not such a badass after all—just an ordinary woman, with all the hopes, dreams, vulnerabilities, and fears that come as I try to navigate my life. I think I always knew that. Maybe it's why I could never fully own what had happened to me.

I think deep inside I knew that this was the beginning of dangerous concessions, concessions that nibble around the edges of your authentic self, eventually taking bigger and bigger bites until the you that is you disappears. So how did I, with my rebel heart, cave? Well, the honest answer is, there would not have been a very lucrative multiyear contract without this concession. In the influencer business, multiyear, long-term partnerships are the gold standard. Otherwise, you cobble together one-off posts on Instagram, taking home a couple thousand dollars after paying everyone you need to pay. This takes a lot of time for very little reward. I still had a few years where I had to generate income until I hit seventy and would start collecting Social Security. Most of my social work jobs did not include a pension, so I had to start building one for myself much later in life. I was forty-seven when I began a retirement account. Long-term partnerships presented me with a conflict and a tradeoff. They provide financial security, in that you are guaranteed a set income over a period of time, so you can be more thoughtful about saying yes or no to other jobs that come your way. Posts for these partners can be planned in advance and generally have a consistent theme, making them much less work than one-off posts. The conflict is that you always have to give up some level of control. The tradeoff is you live with much less anxiety and stress.

This year, I scored several of these partnerships, though only one of them was with a fashion brand. Honestly, at first, they left me with a sense of great relief. Because of them, this year I would make more money than I had ever made in my entire life. Because I was terrified, while other influencers were spending money to reinvest in their business, every penny I made went into the bank. The following year, I would discover that this was the best business decision I ever made.

There are so many parts of Accidental Icon that make me feel like a hamster running on a wheel: the constant engagement with social media, the unpredictable nature of the income, the relentless stream of emails and meetings to be "out there." There are massive amounts of images and information to consume. My organic, see-what-happens approach, while successful to a point, is no longer workable. My little homegrown project to express my creativity and write has become a business. My agent suggests I hire an assistant, a commercial photographer, and a videographer to capitalize on the trends that suggest video content is king. I need to hire a designer for a media kit. I should have a "staff." Unlike my fellow influencers, who intended their projects to be a business, I did not. Despite this, I have become successful. I feel guilty that somehow I am not completely over the moon about this. I feel guilty when I complain to Calvin about not feeling pleasure because of my great privilege in having all that I have. I think all the time of those I worked with in my past career as a social worker.

There are still times I enjoy what I am doing. I am sixty-six, and I am visible and successful. Accidental Icon has given me a voice and visibility, and I know to be grateful for her to that. Producing quirky, humorous little videos about me and a purse for a fashion brand like Kate Spade is fun and creative. The purse is called the Margaux satchel. I've done three of these now, each one with a different color bag. Through the magic of green screen, I become small, and my bag becomes a giant trampoline. In another I am large, and the bag is tiny. I pop it in my mouth like a chocolate. I have a relationship with the creative team, and it's one I value. Most times, I absolutely love to travel, so to get paid for that is another gift I know to appreciate. It's just that my blog self and my Instagram self are moving so far apart, I feel in danger of falling into the ever-widening chasm between. Ever since I lost my website and left academia, it feels like the center will not hold.

I did have a job this year that brought me great pleasure, one where my selves, for a moment, became aligned. I flew to Iceland for a campaign for a fashion brand, and it was one of those perfect experiences where all my desires could come together.

I love the designer; we have many things in common; she is generous, direct, and honest. She treats me to a stay at the

Blue Lagoon Resort, a luxurious spa. Even though I am here to work, she wants me to take a dip in healing and restorative waters. We relax together and talk about having and starting a business in older life.

I love the clothes she picks, the story being told, the setting, and, in this case, the photographer. Watching him work is like taking a master class in composition and design. It is a meditation on details, the tiniest ones, like the placement of a rose, the addition of a glass of whiskey, the choice of a piece of art. Every detail contributes to the story. And although there was much preparation beforehand, like scouting locations, developing the mood, there is also a willingness to take advantage of unplanned but delicious moments, like the model stuffing pizza in her mouth. The capture somehow becomes an art shot. There are photos of me spontaneously smiling. I did not have to be told to do that, a thing many photographers have unsuccessfully tried to make me do during other photo shoots.

I love when there is a narrative that goes with a job I am doing. When people have actually gotten who I am and thought about how we can tell an interesting story together. When this happens, I experience myself as being a creative, not a salesperson. Commerce and beauty do not have to be mutually exclusive when there is art, collaboration, and creativity involved. After all, fashion should always be about aspiration and desire. I lean into the experience and perform the story of a certain woman: the woman who the designer, the photographer, and I all conjure up in our dreams. Here it's a woman in love with the natural world.

There are many pictures of me in deep communion with nature. In one photo I have a fisherman's hat on and am standing at the water's edge, head tilted back. I am deeply inhaling the salty air. My eyes are closed, my arms crossed in front to hug myself. I can see the pleasure I feel in the expression on my face. In another, I stand in tall rain boots in front of a waterfall. I climb a misty mountain holding a wide black umbrella over my head. I run along the shore, my skirt billowing in the wind, arms thrown open, embracing it all. The following year, there would be a quarantine. I would go weeks without experiencing the company of nature. During this shoot I feel reconnected to my body and experience large doses of pleasure.

The designer loves what I write on my blog and wants me to script the copy for this campaign. I am in heaven, given this opportunity to write. I write about garments that allow me to perform a hidden or formerly unarticulated persona. There is a photo of me in a bright pink dress lying on a bed of green moss. Looking at the photo, the designer tells me that I remind her of what people in Iceland call "hidden people," who look and behave like humans but live in a parallel world. In Iceland, they believe in hidden people, elves, and otherworldly creatures. Perhaps my friend's belief in these other worlds allows her to see the possibilities in this one. Perhaps it allowed her to see what was happening to me: that I too was living in a parallel universe.

Over dinner I hear the photographer speak sadly of how little room currently exists for trusting his creative direction and judgment by those who hire him now. It makes him feel like quitting. He reveals how much he loves working with this woman, now my friend, who gives him complete creative freedom, and how wise a decision that is when one sees the results. In some ways, while I hear him talk about the trajectory of his long career as a photographer, the word *bureaucratization* comes to mind. Those who hire him now take away his individual professional discretion, decision-making, and distinctive personality in the alleged service of efficiency. As the sociologist Max Weber maintained, this creates an "iron cage," a technologically ordered, rigid, and dehumanizing kind of work. Why would fashion want to do that to itself?

I completely understand what the photographer is talking about. It's amazing how many people want to write your copy, tell you how to do your photo, and dictate what goes on your site and your social media. Algorithms exert another layer of control. Algorithms are just another set of rules that control what you see and what you must do if you want to be seen. They, like bureaucracy, are another way to manage and govern, except that they are not transparent and do not appear in a policy and procedures manual. This gives you no tangible target to aim your rebellion at. I had sensed I needed to rebel against something; I just could not see or feel what it was. There is a predictable malady experienced by those who work in a bureaucracy, and I feel it coming on now. I've suffered with it before as a social worker. While it feels familiar, this time it's different.

"I got nothing," I say to my blog readers. I tell them not to be kind. Hoping to find inspiration, I log on and review several fashion-oriented web platforms. There seems to be a frenzied desperation in the articles, which are devoid of creativity, depersonalized in a way. Engaging with this content makes me feel a little desperate too. Problematically, when you are too engaged in these kinds of thoughts, there is no room left for inspiration to come into your brain and plant new seeds. What gets planted instead is obsession.

What has become disconcerting is that most of what these web platforms write about is how to make money or, conversely, how not to fade away, like department stores, for example. My favorite of favorites, Barneys, bites the dust. When I retired from teaching, I soothed my anxiety about the unknown by saying, "Worst-case scenario, I can always work at Barneys and still be around beautiful clothes." That imagined safety net is gone. I'm sitting at the only uncluttered spot in my typically small New York City apartment: a tiny corner of my kitchen island. All around me are racks of clothes—woolens, cottons, sequined silks, and sheers in every color of the rainbow. Somber blacks and whites join their more colorful counterparts, spilling out from the bedroom and the three available closets. There are boxes all over my apartment containing clothes and beauty products; I have not had time to open them, much less wear, use, or create inspiring content about their contents. I feel ashamed as I remember the emerging designers at the market shows who cared so much about sustainability, who I wrote about because I believed in sustainability too. I remember how when I first began this project, both in my life and in the photos I took for my blog, all I ever wore was vintage or recycled clothing, and now I am wearing only new clothes. Clothes that, because they are not special to me, will probably be thrown away. It dawns on me that all the boxes and packaging are such a waste. I think of the impact on the environment. I push these thoughts away.

Symbols of my life as a social media influencer, these boxes, these things, are taking up all the living and breathing room in what used to be an open space. I've retreated to my corner, communicating only through my phone and maniacally scrolling through Instagram for hours. Emails come at all times of the day and night, faster than I can answer them. Texts are ringing bells and swooshing back and forth. Constant sounds stress the urgency and the immediacy of responding. The blue light of the phone is always in my face and steals my sleep. I torture myself through the night, my mind playing endless loops:

You had one great idea, you'll never have another.

You're old news, a one-hit wonder.

The world's so bad. How are you helping?

You're so privileged. How dare you be this miserable!

What were you thinking when you gave the dean that resignation letter? You can't even work at Barneys anymore!

Although I'm churning out content and making money, it somehow provides no comfort or satisfaction. I've over-structured and overscheduled my day with apps that are supposed to help me achieve my life goals, but in reality, keeping up with all they are asking me to do or listen to is more exhausting than helpful. I'm running around attending every event and meeting I'm invited to, without thinking for a moment why I should.

The rare moments when I'm not doing these things, I feel guilty and bad. It's as if I float above myself, looking at someone I don't recognize below. I look in the mirror and am distressed at what looks back. My face is haggard and drawn, my hair stringy, my skin and eyes dull. My nails are splitting from too many manicures. I'm irritable and impatient. I snap at the people I love. I stress-eat things that are not even remotely natural. All these things concern me. Not because I want to be beautiful, but because I want to be healthy.

When I was in training to be a psychotherapist, my supervisor was a classically trained psychoanalyst. After each session I conducted with a client, I had to free-write everything I remembered about the session and bring it in to supervision. According to psychoanalytic theory, what I was unconsciously feeling about my client would come out in the notes, just as if I was free-associating while lying on an analyst's couch. My supervisor was masterful at identifying the subtle and unstated emotions that I was not aware of in my work with clients but that appeared in the notes. It amazed me what she could find in a particular word I used to describe an interaction, what I might have left out. A British analyst I greatly admire, Christopher Bollas, coined the term *unthought known* for those experiences that are known, but about which we are not yet able to think. I laugh when I reflect on what my supervisor would have seen that I did not if she read my blog posts from this time. It's all there. When I lost control, how I lost control, my despair about it. Everything is documented in my blog, things both said and unsaid. Maybe I use writing this way because of my training, or maybe it's because that's what writers do. They let what wants to come out come out. They let the story write itself.

In January 2019, Anne Helen Petersen's BuzzFeed article "How Millennials Became the Burnout Generation" went viral. In it, Petersen argues that millennials are subject to social, technological, and economic pressures that threaten to overwhelm the nervous system and wear out coping mechanisms. The article hit a nerve: I now had a name for what I was feeling. Some aspects of my current case of burnout are the same as those when I was a social worker, but others are different. The difference is about the speed and nature of technology and what it does to our bodies and brains. It's when you find that the job of your dreams and fantasies doesn't feel at all like you thought it would.

Our capacity for pleasure makes us human and is important for healthy psychological functioning. Not being able to experience pleasure is actually a clinical condition, called anhedonia. Overwork, financial problems, boring activities, recent tragedies, and even the weather can cause this state. And yes, it's a symptom of burnout too. My writing has always been immediate, urgent, surfacing what I am really preoccupied with in the moment. I enjoy writing without rules, which is probably why I hate academic writing and prefer journaling and blogging. Writing for me is like dreaming, except I am awake. When I return after a time to something I wrote, I am always amazed to see how unaware I was in the moment of writing, despite all those years of analysis and training.

At the same time I experienced these anxieties, I became obsessed with writing a book proposal. Somehow I felt that this is what would save my life. I just couldn't seem to get it right. My agent had already rejected two versions, and I was waiting to hear about the third. The day the call came, I was annoyed; the ringing of the phone had interrupted my scrolling. I saw it was my literary agent. We had a brief conversation. I put down my phone and cried, huge, gulping sobs, and I'm not a crier. Sitting on the floor, bent over in a protective crouch, I felt kicked in the gut.

That moment was extremely painful, yet when I later retrieve that proposal to review while writing this book, rather than hysterically crying, I howl with laughter. In that moment I am the supervisor: I can easily ferret out the subtle clues, the unstated emotions. In the overview, here's what I wrote: "Although technically a boomer, for the last five years I've been working a millennial job. I'm now what's known as an 'influencer.' This new occupation of mine, despite having many exciting perks and aspects I love, has also made me susceptible to a particular affliction known as 'millennial burnout.'" The book was going to be about how I got this burnout, how I recognized that I had it, and what I was going to do to get myself out of it. While my agent didn't think the book was marketable, since so many millennials were already writing about burnout, that proposal was telling my story. It documented my lived experience. It contained my unthought knowns.

Burnout is an occupational phenomenon that affects our health, a state of chronic, unmitigated stress. While experiencing it, we are in a state of emotional, physical, and mental exhaustion. While this is a phenomenon, not a medical condition, the wellness industry, technology entrepreneurs, workplaces, medical practitioners, and therapists have all rushed in, generating a whole new, but not really new, crop of products, hacks, apps, and services. They will not provide a cure. Better self-care is often prescribed as an antidote, but it won't fix the problem, because the problem does not lie within us. The problem is created by how we are expected to work and how our society defines being "productive."

Throughout my career as a professional social worker, I

experienced burnout. But I found ways to recover from it by imaginatively redesigning my work, and in the end felt more resilient than most because of it. This process almost always involved taking on an activity that took me out of my mind and into my body. Rather than take a continuing education course on a topic specifically related to my work, I would take a class that at first glance had nothing to do with it.

For most of my career I worked with young women and mothers who had experienced trauma. Since so much of trauma and burnout is experienced in and through the body, the classes I most often gravitated to were those in the expressive arts. I found myself returning often to classes in acting and improvisation. In these classes I had to engage with my body. Having to improvise stretches your imagination, makes use of what you have on hand at the moment, and sparks spontaneity.

Somehow these embodied experiences would enter into my work, helping me reconfigure it in creative and interesting ways. For example, classes in improvisation and the theater of the oppressed found their way into my work training staff and foster parents about sexual abuse. I worked with a theater group to create scenarios of interactions that often went wrong between staff and adolescents because of a lack of knowledge of how sexual abuse might impact a child. A facilitator would stop the action of the scene and invite the audience to engage with the characters, establishing a dialogue that allowed some distance from the strong emotions generated in interactions like this. After both parties had a greater understanding of each other and why they responded as they had, they had an opportunity to redo the interaction in a more positive way.

These improvisational skills later found their way into my classroom. I ran simulated groups and had students practice challenging interactions with "actor" clients. I might put my notes aside and respond to a student comment that was not on topic but that I knew would provide a moment of great learning. This skill at thinking on my feet was with me during the creation of Accidental Icon. I let myself just be in the moment and improvise as I went along. I let myself experience how the clothes felt on my body when it came to deciding what to wear. These experiences brought a renewed energy and creativity back to my practice that propelled me forward until—inevitably, given the nature of my work—the next episode of burnout came. Other times I would take a creative writing class where I could write about my experiences and process them in a short story or a performance piece. Or it would be a photography class that allowed me to see something from a different angle.

Because they are embodied, I carry these skills with me into whatever work I choose to take on. The expressive skills I learned throughout my life are part of the garments I wear and the garments I take apart. This impulse to reinvent and the skills I learned in my improv classes are how I survived and thrived as a social worker for forty-five years. They are how and why I became the Accidental Icon in the first place.

Now I tell myself I can do it again; it's just a different form of "bureaucracy." This thought steadies me.

One day, exhausted, I just stop. I lie down on my couch. Eyes closed, I give in to the weariness I've been keeping at bay, like a wolf at my door that now threatens to devour me. When I open my eyes, I am scared of being buried alive under the weight of all those clothes in my apartment. With that realization, I have an overwhelming impulse to go to my sewing kit. I want to pull out my seam ripper and take all those garments apart, piece by piece. Somehow I know, because I've done it before, that this will make my life mine again.

67

Learn to Do Improv

'm at work with my seam ripper again. I'm slowly and deliberately taking apart the "garments" I've worn: professor, social worker, Accidental Icon. The embellishments on the fabric are the skills I've learned along the way. I discover what parts of each garment remain true and right, and which no longer fit. I consider what parts of each I love and what parts I do not.

The professor loves teaching, researching, and experiments. She does not like rules about what to teach, or how to teach it. She does not love academic writing. The social worker loves the principle of social justice that is the cornerstone of this profession, the hope and resilience she sees in her clients, and the practice-guiding principle that highlights the importance of understanding a person in light of the various contexts in which that person lives. The social worker does not like systems that are set up to help her clients but frequently treat them in unfair and unequal ways, or the way this profession can do harm when it tries to do good. The influencer loves traveling, meeting new people, learning new things, clothes, and writing a blog that inspires others. She does not like selling things, wasting clothes and cardboard boxes, and spending hours on social media.

So now that I know what I know and have somewhat recovered my senses, the question becomes "What now?"

It is January 2020, the beginning of a new year. Like so many others, when another year begins, I formulate goals. I am determined to set up a healthy routine and construct a gentler work life. I'm doing research and reading to help me understand what happened to me so it does not happen again. I read books like *How To Do Nothing: Resisting the Attention Economy* by Jenny Odell and *Trick Mirror: Reflections on Self-Delusion* by Jia Tolentino. When burned out in the past or needing to heal because of something that hit me hard, I've always figured out a new way to recover. The times this happened to me before are memories that come alive with sights, sounds, smells, people, and places, each a richly textured brocade of an episode of repair, renewal, and reinvention. I remember when I took my Building a Vintage Business class. In the two months before the pandemic hits New York City and the world as I know it changes, I have experiences like this again. I have recovered memories I thought were lost to me. I find pleasure, joy, inspiration, and a sense of purpose from these encounters. I find myself once again in an "improv class."

I receive an email from a group of Parsons Fashion Design and Society MFA students who have been given the assignment to make a collection for "seniors." The course involves creating designs for wearers who are disabled, plus-size, transgender, and/or aging. They divide students into four teams, with each team charged to find a muse/collaborator within the respective category. This is to ensure primary research and a meaningful outcome. The students ask me for an interview, hoping that I might become their muse. I am beyond delighted; one insight I have gained from my recent episode of seam ripping is how much I miss my students, and teaching.

The students have gone around to senior centers, asking what older people want in their clothing. The answers discourage them, coming more around issues of fit, comfort, and disguising signs of age. Though these elements are important, the students seem to want an aesthetic of age that can inspire them to go beyond the now. They want to make old age high fashion, something beyond just function. I think these fashionable young people want to design clothes they can see themselves in when they grow old. As we speak together, the fluid, internal experience of age, the memories held, and the desire to evoke them in what we wear are topics they become animated and excited about. Along with their tutors, these students and I begin our work together. Bespoke textiles, photos, drawings, prototypes, and a multitude of other imaginings spring into the room. The process starts with me bringing in pieces from my wardrobe that hold meaning for me. There is the Yohji Yamamoto suit I wore to my first day of class and a Fashion Week event. There is an oversize burnt-orange coat that covers me like a blanket, which I wear when I want to feel warm and safe. There is a paisley Indian-print dress I wore in the 1970s and now throw on when I go to the beach. Its colors are faded, and the thin cotton fabric is almost transparent after being worn for so many years. It seems on the brink of disintegration. There is the sleeveless A-line dress with pastel-green and purple flowers that I wore under my doctoral gown the day that I received my PhD. We have many conversations about the experiences attached to clothing during different periods of my life. We discuss how what I wore now, or wanted to wear, could allow experiences from different times of my life to be remembered. My young friends are curious about how I came to be empowered to wear what I want, resist trends, use clothes as devices to tell my personal stories, and see style as being unique to every person.

I share with them how Calvin and I were recently walking around Harlem, taking photos, and came upon the only remaining Kangol hat store in the world. I'm not a hat person at all, but I had a Kangol beret I used to wear backward with overalls and a velvet shirt silkscreened with Our Lady of Guadalupe when I was first exploring my creative self in the early 1990s, right after I left my marriage and was about to turn forty. The Our Lady of Guadalupe shirt was a nod to my preoccupation with Frida Kahlo after a trip to Mexico, growing up Catholic, and Latin dancing, which I was learning and practicing every weekend. But I digress.

The point here is, when I walk into that store, I am transported back to that time. I hear the music and remember the galleries I went to, the classes I took, and the books I read. So I try to explain to the students that it's not that I need to wear exactly what I wore then, but clothes that evoke the feelings and memories I felt. An approach to style that comes from our unique identities can convey a sense of time and place far more eloquently than a copy of something already worn. An article of clothing or an accessory like a Kangol cap contains history; it is a device that can tell a story, one that is as different as the people who put it on. As the person our age managing the Kangol store said, "Rappers, hipsters, nerds, and church ladies all wear Kangol caps."

The students and I speak a good deal about what it means to be old. Each week I arrive for a fitting of what they design, and the tutors give a critique. This becomes a conversation about how bodies change as we age. The students make adaptations. Creating the garments and adjustments made to the patterns and design mirrored the changes and accommodations that I make as I get older.

The tutors and I observe how stereotypes and preconceived notions about being old find their way into the sessions, giving us the opportunity to question them. The tutors observe how the students' initial designs cover me completely, not acknowledging that I might still be a sexual being. By default, clothing for older adults is made to cover up their aging bodies. After this conversation, the textiles become more transparent, though they remain respectful. I learn from these young creatives how to transform a concept into a garment. The more assumptions fall away, the more stereotypes are challenged, the more creative the students become. There is a heightened communication between the students and myself; we are deeply engaged. I feel a return to myself. New textiles need to be designed from old ones—or, you could say, improvised—as none exist that, standing alone, represent this new concept of being old.

Usually garments made for aging bodies are not modern or representative because they don't take into consideration the disconnect between the internal experiences of older people and the reality of their physical bodies. Internally, age is a fluid experience. Many older people still feel youthful and engaged. My body may be disintegrating, but the designers turn this process into textiles that show how beautiful it can be. They recycle textiles and work with scraps of fusible interfacing and other materials found around the workroom. The clothes are not retro but modern, and they convey the sexuality and rebellious spirit that still inhabits me. This results in the production of garments incorporating intricately crafted bespoke textiles, like a dress made of crocheted paisley prints in oranges and earth tones. There are suggestions of the body beneath. The students create a black coat with visible layers of varying tones and textures of gray and shaped like a cocoon that opens to reveal a transparent shirt. Pants and tunic with green and purple flowers caught in a spiderweb knit. These are garments that turn remembering and aging into something that is modern and new, and not just a retrospective view of a long life.

As a way of giving back to the students who have given so much to me, I arrange an event hosted in a space that serves as a launchpad for emerging designers. I want to thank them. During our time together, I once again experienced the joy of teaching. I remembered the hope, inspiration, and encouragement I received from emerging, unknown designers when I first started my blog, and how they found their way into my photographs and writing. I felt again the excitement of learning something new and never explored before. Along with the students, I was researching and writing as the project emerged, activities that bring me enormous pleasure. I became connected to my body again and anchored in the present moment. We were together in a kind of improv class, because improvisation was at the heart of it; that is what the students, their tutors, and I did together as we created these new clothes. Each outfit created became a scene that performed a story of a life, each garment a narrative that revealed some secrets about how to be old. At that time of my life, these were stories I very much needed to hear.

I invite a well-known designer friend and other high-profile people in fashion who are now on my contact list. The clothing is on display, as well as the students, and I speak about our experience and what we learned from working together. For the students, understanding the developing nature of identity as opportunity, deconstructing standardized notions of the "ideal" body, and understanding that the internal experience of aging is fluid are gifts they took away from the process. In their designs, they layered years of memory and meaning and saw aging in a way that was additive, not subtractive, and something to look forward to. In their hands, aging became richly layered, full of different textures, colors, and shapes. The clothes the students designed for me make me feel understood. Working with younger people and solving this problem together reminds me of the utility of intergenerational collaboration, deep listening, and mutual respect. Can you imagine, if we worked together so creatively on the multitude of issues we face in this current time, how we might change the way we think about being old or young?

Another Parsons student duo with an interest in textiles wants to meet me. The students are interested in not just creating something new but preserving the old. In other words, they are studying the artisan traditions of textile making. They feel, they say, that they are being discouraged from pursuing anything not "innovative and new." This leads to a discussion of what is meant by innovation. I asked them to pull out their phones and look up the word's dictionary definition, which includes the phrase "a change made to an existing product, idea, or field." I encourage the students to focus on this as their mission as they think of what their professor told them.

Nothing is ever completely new; there is always a seed from the past. So I share with these two young women all the sights, sounds, epiphanies from a trip I just made to Paris, courtesy of Hermès. Hermès is the perfect case study to teach about craftsmanship, tradition, history, upcycling of ideas, luxury, and reinvention. Production is limited, and

items purchased are often passed from generation to generation, and in this way are sustainable. These are attributes the
company has maintained since 1837. Hermès is still a family-
owned business. It resists being acquired or displaced.

The Hermès trip was a redo of my previous trip to Paris.
This time I had no reason to rush home. Every experience
planned for me and the other invited influencers provided
inspiration, learning, and engagement. While our travel and
hotel were paid for, there were no expectations for us to promote anything, or even that we would post at all.

Thankfully my time in Paris with Hermès provided un-
forgettable experiences, because I didn't know it then, but it
would be the last time I'd travel for a very long time.

I find myself on the rue du Faubourg-Saint-Honoré, an ex-
tension of the street I walked the last time I was here. This
time I am high above Paris on a rooftop that is the site of an
exquisite, secret garden. This is the building that contains
the original Hermès factory. It's February 2020, and I guess
you could say I am at the top of my game. Working with a
brand that has the stature of Hermès is the epitome of influencer success.

The lunch is buffet style, served on Hermès china. There
are sugar cubes shaped in the letter H. After lunch, we de-
scend floor by floor, and on each, a host provides us with a
piece of the company's history. On one floor, they continue
to make saddles and harnesses in the same way they did in

1880. On another are books of photos: images of custom orders of whatever fantasy made in leather a customer may have. There are bags that look like a green apple, boxing gloves, a car, and airplane seat covers. We learn of the research that goes into bringing designs like this to life. On the next floor are tables, a craftsperson at each. One person makes each Hermès bag. The company encourages workers to innovate in a design-thinking way, and they are often the ones to name a product. Strewn around the tables are pieces of leather that, when sewn together, will become a Kelly or a Birkin.

All bags are entirely hand-stitched, and Hermès uses saddle stitch, a traditional harness-making method, to join the leather components of each bag. Our guide leads us to a nearby room. Here, on a table, are multicolored spools of thread, pieces of leather, hammers, snips, blocks of beeswax, and large wooden tongs to hold the leather in place while it is stitched. A craftsperson shows us how to use two needles and a single piece of thread as we make stitches in our pieces of leather. When done by a master, every stitch is precisely the same size and tightness. Later we learn how to hammer the stitches into neat lines until they are smooth.

Although we could not make an additional trip to Lyon, where the Hermès silk scarves are made, we visit an Hermès store that contains an archive of scarves, silks, and other objects. There are books with pages that contain strips of silk in every existing color. In the center is a table set with sparkling china and cutlery designed by the house, waiting for our dinner later in the evening. I forget I am in a store; there are moments when I feel I am in a museum, a theater, or a restaurant. The ways this space can be endlessly reimagined remind me again of my improv classes. The store becomes a third space, one where anything can happen when you fill it with creative people. It is a site of reimagining that encourages reuse.

We are shown the first red handbag ever made by the brand, in Rouge H, an emblematic color for the house. It's a dark red with a hint of brown. There is a pair of tan leather gloves that contains a secret message to a lover. The words—in French, of course—are scattered amid bouquets of orange flowers, and embroidered along the back of each thumb. Object after beautiful object shows evolution and adaptation over time. Like me, they are the same but different.

In another section there are perfumes, jewelry, and finally lipstick, the reason we are here. At a reception where we try the new lipstick, the makeup artist chooses the color known as Rouge H for me. I am happy; it is the most elegant shade of red. Suddenly I feel like the woman who hung off that fire escape years ago. I feel every single sense being activated. After the last year of being disconnected from my body and the depersonalization that occurred when I was so burned out, I am once again centered in the present moment. No longer anxious and stressed, I can reside for a time in the unknown.

A trip to Versailles, while lovely, does not come close to the pleasure I feel as I once again experience all the elements I love about fashion. While I didn't have to, I bought a silk

174 — HOW TO BE OLD

scarf of my own and posted about my experiences because I was so ecstatic. The PR person later reported to my agent that my engagement level exceeded that of all other invited guests. I am sure the reason is that I had not only found my way back to Paris; I'd found my way back to my authentic self. I remembered why I started to be Accidental Icon to begin with.

The experiences I had working with the Parsons students and my trip to Paris with Hermès make me remember what I love about fashion in the first place: its history, its craftsmanship, its ability to constantly reinvent, how it can tell stories. I find in these experiences a renewed purpose for my work as Accidental Icon. I have stopped trying to control what that work will be; I feel ready to step on a stage, meet some new actors, and find out what may emerge. I've strengthened my improvisational muscles. My body remembers. The people I meet, the conversations we have, the ideas we play with, where we travel to, how we manage our feelings along the way, and what we discover about living as humans in this current social, economic, and technological age—these are what I want my work to be about.

Before I have a chance to conjure up exactly what that might be, the pandemic hits New York.

My blog followers and I decided years ago to name the state that precedes a reinvention What Nowness. It implies satisfaction with whom we are at our core, that this state of not knowing is normal, and it can be a precursor to a fresh burst of creative self-expression. It is a state of perpetual openness to whatever may come before you, whenever and however it appears. I have returned, during this time of the coronavirus, full circle to the question and the same state of uncertainty: the not knowing; the unformed "ness" of it, this time more urgent, more critical, and more pressing than ever before. All the fault lines and cracks in bold relief. It's as if Mother Nature has sent us naughty children to our rooms to have a deep think about our bad behavior. In these rooms, we do become childlike again, using our imaginations, re-sourcefulness, and creativity to meet our needs. Dare I say we have time to reflect again? This is where I find hope.

I am in my apartment, remaining safe and healthy, as my beautiful city suffers unspeakable loss. New York is manifest-ing unparalleled heroism from first responders and medical personnel. The kindness and generosity manifested by those in my local community have been a balm. Neighbors check in on us. Our favorite small and homey local restaurant makes food for those of us in my neighborhood who would gather there before this happened, and for those working tirelessly in the large, looming hospital just a few blocks away. We say thanks to the pharmacists and grocery workers putting themselves and their families at risk to provide ser-vice to the community, to earn an income for their families. It makes me feel sick inside to think about how I took them for granted before, now that their jobs require so much sac-rifice and danger. A fashion designer friend who is in danger of losing his own business hops on his bicycle, in answer to a call I put out on social media, to deliver masks to child welfare workers who still must go into homes and homeless shelters to make sure families and children are safe.

As the months of the pandemic go on, Calvin and I are learning to cherish connection to family and friends, reconnecting with gardens and nature, cooking, being kind, helping others, and using social media for networking, for social action, and to express our humanness. I vow that my mother, daughter, and granddaughter will always come before anything I may do as Accidental Icon. There will be no more missed birthday parties, no weeks between visits to my mom. More time for babysitting. As this goes on and we do not know for how much longer, already enough time has passed for these refound behaviors to become habits. Underneath it all, there is an incredible potential to change how we live as a community, how we treat the earth and others, and how we relearn an ethic of care. There has never been a more important time to ask "What now?" The pandemic has pushed me to a place I have never been before. One where I must call upon every skill of improvisation I have ever learned.

My apartment is small. The number of garments hanging on racks in multiple rooms makes it look as if I've been living in an exclusive boutique rather than a home. Since the moment everything stopped, the pandemic has forced me to confront the economic vulnerability of my new occupation. There will not be money coming in the way it did last year. The clothes are in my face, tickling my nostrils at the very moment I'm feeling a need to take deep and cleansing breaths. This time I do not push the shame I feel about having so many of them away.

Yet I can't imagine a world without beautiful garments. I would be like a painter without paint or a photographer without a camera. It's always been the way I express who I am, how I rebel, how I make a statement. But what has become so very clear now, if it was not before, is that my (and our) relationship with clothing will need to change in this new world. I need to move beyond the surface aesthetic and find out the values that really make clothes beautiful. How can we embed values in the filaments of their textiles that are respectful of the earth and those who make them? That is enough to take a chance on, to collect as an asset, to know they will be something I can pass to future generations. Articles of clothing that I can endlessly reimagine. That I will not throw away. My meandering and lazy what-now daydreams, my recovered memory of what I value and what's important to me, the experiences I had in the beginning of this year before the pandemic about how I might move forward—it all takes on heightened meaning now. There is a greater urgency to answer it. To find my way.

In conversations on Instagram, I find there are so many women like me who are feeling ambivalent about their relationship with clothes in this moment. It seems superficial, considering what is happening to the world, but for some of us, what we wear is a second language. Despite all the magic I imbue my garments with, they are still material objects. Objects that in the making have caused so much harm to the earth in the Time Before Corona.

We see it in the broken supply chains that are more than just canceled orders. For many who work in factories in Bangladesh and other faraway places, canceled orders could mean no food and work. Our favorite stores have laid off their employees. Those who style and take beautiful pictures of clothing go quiet. And those who, like me, write about clothing are no longer paid for our words.

I realize during this time that the decisions we make about fashion can profoundly change the world for the good. The fashion system has been brought to its knees, and how it gets up is in our hands. I can choose to wear what can become an activist instrument, one that not only expresses who I am but is also adorned with my values. There is a quiet dignity in that decision.

One of the silver linings I find during the Time During Corona is that I am making do with less, in part because I *want* to. In the space of having less, there is more room for imagination and creativity, more room to find a way into my daily routine and back into my apartment. There is a reckoning with what is really important. We are now at the heavy, solid base of that pyramid of basic needs. Our lives are being threatened. The integrity of our physical bodies, our need for food, how we think of the word *shelter*, our yearning for the connected, tactile human touch of those we cannot be with—it's all at risk. Bizarrely, even toilet paper is hard to find. While we have been in a prolonged process of destroying the purity of the air we breathe, it now contains droplets that are destroying us. Living in cities that are hot-beds of pollution means that if we contract the virus, we are at risk of having a more serious case. It hangs around on all the things we buy.

But in the spring, there are also new plantings in tilled empty gardens, open to new possibilities. Outside my window, nature is still green and blooming despite it all. By the time we finally emerge from our houses, it will already be summer. Some of us who have the privilege of being safe enough to think and reflect will enter this new season with a heightened sense of what is important and what needs to change. For me, as my young neighbors text or knock on my door to see if I need anything, as my favorite local restaurant delivers meals to the hospital three blocks away, as a refrigerator filled with food appears on the street, and as designers help me get and give masks to social workers, I see all the possibilities of small. All the possibilities of local, community-based efforts, and all the innovation that is coming from craft, reinvention, and reuse. In this moment, I see the rebuilding happening from the bottom up, not the top down. It is my local neighborhood that is providing social welfare right now. They are the ones protecting me from risks and insecurities. These are the assets that need to be preserved and strengthened as we move forward. So how do I and the industry I am a part of continue to use clothing as our form of creative expression in ways that promote social well-being, human and ecological flourishing? That embrace the values of small, local, and community-based social welfare? When the world opens up again, can these good intentions be maintained?

I have given the virus a pet name, maybe to control it, to show it's not the boss of me. I call it the "Great Interrupter." Interruptions, while sometimes disruptive, when well-timed can allow us to pause and evaluate what we are doing. I have to say that between the Great Interrupter and Black Lives Matter, I feel like I've checked into a rehab center. This period is a necessary detox from the consumerist social media world, and the need for constant self-promotion I had gotten lost in. The recession that has accompanied the pandemic has had the greatest impact on the service economy, especially the gig economy. Since this is how I now make my living, I have to think carefully about how I want to expend my resources. This brings a newfound appreciation for less, a sharper, clearer perspective on what makes up value and quality, an expanded understanding of luxury.

During my stint in "rehab," I've discovered I can still make a living that will meet my basic needs. I don't need to do more. In truth, I love being less frantic and less busy. I'm consuming less, producing less waste. I am still doing sponsored posts to generate income, but there are way less of them. I give them more thought and attention than before. The captions I post with each picture on Instagram are becoming longer and longer. I find myself mini-blogging on Instagram and macro-blogging on my website. Given the constraints of having to produce content in my apartment and protect my privacy, I've rediscovered how to stretch my creativity within limits. I have had to call on my skills of improvisation repeatedly, with no city streets or trips abroad to inspire a photo. There is only a stark white wall in my apartment as background. It is like the empty room of an improvisation class. I wrap the white towels I am promoting around my body and head to create a gown, put on a long gold earring, and call the sponsored post "Quarantine Couture." On my Instagram feed there are many photos of me in front of the white wall. They show me wearing a veiled hat I got during a trip to Amsterdam; seam ripping a pair of jeans to turn them into a skirt; hiding my face behind fuchsia velvet gloves; wearing an apron dress and sitting with orange tulips. In a nod to my early beginnings, there are a few photos in black and white. Each photo inspires an essay, and I write more blog posts than I have in quite a while. I write about my mother's apron collection, about wanting to be a ballerina, about visiting a café in Amsterdam that was built by my great-grandfather, about pearls and white shirts. Hair, anger, humor, cocktail shakers, and moving slow. How interesting that all the first-class flights, luxury hotels, gourmet meals, expensive clothing, and front-row seats never incited me to write the way I am writing now, when my biggest source of inspiration is a bare white wall.

Living a fashionable life is so much more than the clothes you wear. It's also how you wear your values, experience, and morality. Clothes and other objects that give us pleasure don't have to conflict with values that honor all people and the planet. I now see finding the intersections as a creative challenge. I am finding my way back to a cohesiveness between my two chosen work identities. In the beginning of Accidental Icon, I was a professor of social work and a fashion blogger. These two roles, and all the things I loved about each of them, managed to coexist in harmony, and one informed the other. When I stopped working as a professor, it was as though Accidental Icon lost the part of herself that kept her grounded and in the real world. It feels good to see these two parts of me reunited; I look forward to what they will do together this time around. For the moment, we have all the time in the world to figure it out.

Today I spritzed on what I call my writer's perfume, the one I got the first time I went to Paris. Like garments and accessories, perfume is an evocative object for me. They are all objects that are the carriers of my dreams and imagination. Objects I use to improvise a new story. Objects that help me remember. I've been doing an impressive amount of reading about writing these days. It's almost all I do. During my reinvention times, I usually go back to school. It is no different this time. I think that maybe I should try to get an MFA in creative writing. Since I already have four degrees, I've been a professor for over twenty years, and I know how to construct a syllabus, I decide I probably have what it takes to design my own degree, hence the reading about writing. Because of the quarantine and Zoom, there are new opportunities outside of institutional structures like an MFA program to write with others and workshop what you write. When I'm walking across my six-hundred-square-foot apartment or pacing across my broad, flat roof to get in my twelve thousand steps a day, I'm listening to podcasts about writing. I'm back to being consistent with my blog posting. I experiment with doing some microblogging on Instagram. It seems to go over well. My followers are more interested in ideas and sentiment than "stuff." What I am writing about seems to resonate.

This quarantine has filled me with a need to tell stories. I have come to understand during the past year that the unique look I create with my clothes is not the thing that gives me pleasure; the pleasure comes in sitting down and telling a story about those garments. Until now, my style has been my claim to fame. Now, though, my readers help me believe that it may be more about how I write about the garments and feelings that create that style than the style itself.

Now, during the time of the Great Interrupter, I write more than I have in a very long time. I have always wanted to "be a writer," whatever that means. What I *have* done is actually write. There are countless journals and notebooks, their dated entries spanning years. A dissertation. Papers.

An academic book. Six years of blog posts. I wonder why I don't consider the act of writing across a sixty-plus-year life-span "being a writer." What makes me feel I do not deserve to claim this as part of my identity?

Losing work from my influencer life is giving me more free time than I've had for many years. Not having time has always been the excuse I use when I don't write. It is still tempting to distract myself from what I am working on by picking up my phone, checking email, or looking at Instagram. During this moment I am the one creating an interruption. I have to ask myself why this is so. When I was a child, I was often interrupted by the seemingly insatiable demands of my large family. There were the times when I was reading a book I could not wait to get back to, and my brother needed help with homework. The ballet lessons that ended because there was another mouth to feed. The figure skating lessons that stopped because we moved. But what I must own now is that it is me creating the interruption that takes me away from doing something I love so much. I will give myself some credit: though I might create interruptions, like a homing pigeon, I always find my way back home. I find ways around the disruptions, such as my childhood habit of going back to that favorite book I had to put down after everyone else in the house had gone to bed. Still wary, a part of me waits for someone to turn off the light. However, interruptions will always keep coming, as they do if you live an engaged life. You just can't let them entice you away from doing the thing you most wish for. When will I ever learn this? How much time will I let go by before I do? It hits me hard: there is no longer all the time in the world.

The Great Interrupter is interrupting life for so many in such devastating ways, causing losses of life and livelihood at almost incomprehensible levels. I'm always holding this larger reality, while at the same time I manage the still-privileged reality of my own interrupted life. It's untenable for me, and disrespectful to others, to waste anything I have right now. So the phone is going into another room when I sit down to write. I will skim headlines only. I will stop being the Great Interrupter of my writing life.

Just when I think I'm done, that I've resolved all my issues and am clear on my priorities and ready to move ahead, there are times life tells me, "Oh no you don't." There is still something I am missing, still something more to learn. Just when I feel safe, like I've outwitted the enemy, in this case COVID-19, there is something else just around the corner to ambush me. It's the big improvisational game that life plays. However, if you decide to play the game as an active participant, you get much better at thinking on your feet, collaborating with others, and responding creatively to conflict, change, and challenges. After all, what is life anyway but one long, unfolding drama that you are a part of?

During my first trip upstate to visit my daughter after the quarantine ended, a spider bit me. This triggered a series of medical mishaps that led to my becoming quite ill with a serious colon infection. Because I needed proximity to a bathroom, I was once again confined to my apartment. I could not do all the things that distract me from feelings or states I am not yet ready to feel. I could not get up, have yet another cup of coffee. I could not spend time on my phone scrolling on Instagram or going to events to make sure I was still being seen. I was not up to getting dressed, nor to speaking to anyone. As the days ticked by and the initial anxiety about diagnosis and the proper course of treatment passed, I lay in a state of doing absolutely nothing.

No, my colon told me, you are not done yet.

Into the silence that comes with doing nothing arrived the realization that in some ways I probably intended to go on as I did before. I was still doing sponsored posts. Yes, I would do influencer work less; I would be more ethical and work only with sustainable brands. But I would still be doing it. I had to ask myself: In all sincerity, had I really changed? How would I react once the trips, invitations, high-end clothes, and exciting events and opportunities started coming in again? Could I really resist them? It's easy to say you would when the things you say you don't want anymore aren't available anyway.

Despite being strong and healthy in ways that lowered my risk of catching the virus even at my age, this episode of debilitating illness reminded me of the fragility and vulnerability of the human body. It was a premonition of what would inevitably happen to my body as I got even older. I was getting old in a very important moment of historical reckoning. I wanted my life to have meaning. Posting photos of myself using beauty products on Instagram did not seem to rise to the occasion. Not to mention the double message I was sending about owning your age, including your wrinkles, while promoting products that suggest that those fine lines will disappear if only you use them. I open all the packages that come in the mail. I carefully fold the boxes and put them in the recycling bin. I donate the many bottles of creams, shampoos, and nail polish to a homeless shelter that some social work students are working in. I decline offers of more gifts. It seems I am cleaning house, preparing for a move.

Only a fraction of the garments on those racks that fill my space still fit. Somehow the restoration of my body and values is no longer in sync with the city or this apartment in a way that gives me a sense of rightness. I don't want my life to be fraught with anxiety. How I was old during the last two years no longer feels true to the self I remember and the self I have now become. I need a change of scene that will inspire me to improvise a new performance. It's time to really shake things up.

It is the end of June 2020. I have just had a birthday. I am sixty-seven. On this day Calvin cooked dinner for us, a healthy concoction of barley, green beans, scallions, and miso soup designed to help the good flora in my digestive system bloom again. We come together for this meal, transformed through the intense experience we have both lived through. We are the same but different.

Calvin and I are both changed by the many days we spent together during the quarantine, the long months we passed in our small space without being outside. We learned to need and use less, to love fully, and to make use of the gift of time. We have grown even closer, our lives more intertwined than before. He took great care of me when I was ill.

I quite spontaneously and out of the blue instigate an improv game, throwing out a scenario: "We have enough money for a down payment to buy a house and move out of the city." Calvin decides to play: "Are you serious?" Suddenly I find that I am, and he is too. It's amazing how fast this idea takes hold of us. It's hard to imagine that just this very morning, neither of us would have ever thought about making a move. Until now we have been quite happy to rent, a freedom that allowed us to live our urban nomad lifestyle, moving when we felt a need for something new. We even saw our retirement that way. Now we feel a need to be rooted. We've never felt this need before. Perhaps the strong winds that have blown through the world in the form of a pandemic have resulted in this desire. Maybe the fragility and vulnerability I experienced when I was ill made us both realize that we shouldn't wait too long. We keep playing this improv game, and discover that we want to grow our own herbs and vegetables. I want an enormous flower garden, to have fresh flowers in every room. We want to know our neighbors, be closer to my mother, daughter, granddaughter, my sister and brother. We want to fill our house with recycled furniture. A sewing machine, so I can upcycle the clothes that already hang in my closet. A place for Calvin to print his photographs. A place to write and make more things with my hands. And yes, Calvin reminds me, bikes too. We click on Zillow to see what we can find.

———————————

I've been looking at my life differently these days. Somehow, while remaining firmly in the present, I'm better appreciating the beauty of the past. The beauty of what is old. In these ahistorical times, I find that history provides us in hindsight with lessons we would be wise to remember right now. The constant push for "newness" that is part of fashion, the speed of technology, the Instagram Stories that disappear in twenty-four hours only to be replaced with another new thing—they crash over my head like a wave and make me yearn for something old. There's a comfort in solid, well-made things from the past that have echoes of craftsmanship and care. Perhaps that is why I've gotten the idea that we must buy an old house. Perhaps after this past year's experience, I am comfortable with the thought of buying something that needs to be restored, like I do. Something that needs some renovation.

The city is slowly coming back awake. We can go out now. We take the train to our appointments with our realtor. We are being prudent; we have a budget that takes into account that sometime in the next few years we will be living on a fixed income. We check on the availability and quality of nearby medical facilities. We want to live in a diverse environment, preferably one with other creative people. It's hard in a very inflated real estate market not to become discouraged. One of the houses we are interested in provokes a bidding war, and we do not wish to compete. We can wait.

I am starting to get more work. Yes, I am still an influencer. But in my mind, it's temp work until I can find a better full-time gig. This time I'm aware of what I am doing and why I am doing it. Although I really need a manicure right now, as I look down at my hands, they still look strong; they have a lot more to do. I've gone months without a manicure, and my nails are healthier and stronger. As my fingers are running over my computer's keyboard, they are telling me they want to dance with a needle as they did in that Paris workshop, spend time in the dirt, maybe even take up embroidery, something I loved as a child. I give them all a nod but also let them know: All in good time. At this moment, we are writing a post. That is more than enough. We can wait.

There is a small city ten minutes away from where my daughter lives. It is in the midst of a revival. It sits on the bank of the Hudson. Several years ago, as with other Hudson River towns, artists moved here from the city in search of more affordable space. One can feel a creative vibe when walking on Main Street or visiting the local coffee shop, known as the community's living room. There are more than a hundred artists' studios housed in some of the older buildings and former factories. Crayola crayons were invented here, at the Peekskill Chemical Company. When I look up the history of the city, I find that an inventive and entrepreneurial spirit has always been here.

Beautiful yet neglected Victorians and Craftsman homes abound and have been snapped up during the pandemic by young couples from Brooklyn and Queens who appreciate the easy forty-minute train ride into New York and close proximity to hiking trails and bike paths. Calvin will still be commuting to his hospital lab, so this is an important consideration. In the warm weather streets are closed for outdoor dancing and dinner. There is a farmer's market. There is a diverse mix of people who are committed to trying to live harmoniously despite differences. The local government remains skeptical of overzealous developers. It is here, in this place that is renewing and restoring, tucked away on a corner lot that borders a nature preserve, that we find our house.

Calvin and I have survived the worst of the pandemic year, and we now find ourselves the owners of a vintage house. Built in 1912, it's quirky and charming. It has many elements that evidence skilled labor and the work of artisans. Like me, it's got some repair, restoration, and renewal to do. But it's the perfect muse for a couple who love to be creative and are "vintage" themselves. We call it our "new/old house," and Calvin dubs us the Vintage Hipsters. I'm curious to see where this leads me. How it will affect my style, the things I post, what I write about. I suspect there will be photos of other things besides me and what I might choose to wear. It reminds me of when I first started my blog and had not a clue where it would take me. But an older but wiser me is more than ready to find out.

68

Make Your House
Your Home

ince I was a small girl, I've imbued objects with magical properties. Perhaps it came from being raised as a very strict Catholic. Because of my faith, I was asked to believe the most incredible things. Bones, minute pieces of cloth, beads, medals, plastic statuettes, palm leaves, ashes, wafers, wine, small gold crosses, and water, through the act of being blessed, could become something more than everyday things. These objects could create miracles, and they fueled my childhood imagination. Even today, if I come across any of these tokens revered in Catholicism, they evoke a strong emotional response, one that I attach meaning to and retrieve memories from.

This tendency of mine appears to border on superstition, but it has made many dull moments and ordinary objects I've encountered in my life infinitely more exciting. By now, you already know how I sometimes project my imaginative tendencies on certain articles of clothing, sunglasses, or red lipstick. In my stories, they always become much more than they really are. When I first step into my new/ old house, I can sense this same old superstitious mysticism taking hold.

When we went to look at houses, I knew I was not looking at the configuration of the house, what architectural style most engaged me, or how many bathrooms there were. I was only looking for signs that we had found the one. I tuned in to how each house made me feel, and saw if I sensed some latent magic.

When I walked in the door of the new/old house, the first thing I saw in the hall was a secretary exactly like the one my grandmother used in her home in Connecticut. Light streamed in from the tall windows in the formal dining room, with its sparkling china and silver place settings. A memory transported me back to the table-manners lessons my grandmother provided in her dining room free of charge. A slipup meant the tap of a silver spoon on the back of your hand. Standing in the dining room of this house, I could almost feel the rap of metal on my skin. There was a stained-glass window by the stairs. I climbed them and walked to the farthest room off the hall. When I first saw the small tower attached to the house, I knew the room at the top would be like all the rooms I imagined a writer laboring in, whenever I passed a house with a tower. Who cared that the master bedroom was small, that the plaster walls needed repair, or that the kitchen needed a complete renovation? That the upstairs bathroom was a horror? I could already see my antique writing desk in front of the three bow windows, along with a comfortable pink velvet chair. Maybe I'd find a chaise to read on.

Outside in the backyard an expanse of green, cut in half by a meandering path of broken concrete, led to towering trees. There were invasive vines, unpruned bushes, and wildflowers all over the lawn. It was the skeleton of an English country garden, and in my imagination, I could already see

the blooms. There were mature hydrangea and rhododen-
dron bushes to get us started, and morning glories already
climbed the wall of the detached garage. It reminded me
of an overgrown secret garden, like the one in my favorite
childhood book. And there behind the garage, tucked in a
corner, was yet another sign: a statue of the Blessed Mother,
who put me in mind of mine. Calvin and I later joked that if
we were lucky enough to get our house within budget amid
the most overheated real estate market people have seen in
years, the statue was staying. My house became magical
before I'd even bought it. I couldn't wait to discover all its
charms and secrets and how they would make my imagination fly. Maybe it wasn't magic. Maybe it's just that I'd always been able to see the potential in things, in people. Even
though there may be times I get stuck, I can always move
beyond what is into what can be.

I'm sixty-eight now, it's November of the year the pandemic
hit, and we've bought an old house. The night of the closing
we sleep on an inflatable mattress. We bring none of the furniture from our old apartment; the black-and-chrome urban
vibe does not fit here. I'm starting to feel like I want some
color in my home. This will be a site of reimagining, reus-
ing, and recycling, like the Hermès store in Paris. Our realtor
started by showing us a number of town houses, the preference of her other customers our age. We did not want a home
that was new and already done; we wanted one that could

become and change as we were. One that had some history. One that had potential. One that would make some demands on us, that would have expectations for us, so we could continue to grow and maintain our health. One that had bones that could hold a long and hopeful future, but within which we could create the kind of home that would provide the opportunity, like a blank white wall, for two creative people to make it their own. A house with magical properties.

While larger than our New York City apartment, this house is still rather modest, coming in at fifteen hundred square feet. It has a low-pitched roof and deep bracketed overhangs. It's made of simple materials: wood, brick, and pebble dash. Described in real estate listings as a "side hall Victorian with Arts and Crafts features," this house is of an architectural style, common in the early 1900s, that was called "transitional." That means it features some of the excesses that were hallmarks of the Victorian style, like the tower room and pocket doors, but also some of the humble and utilitarian trademarks of Arts and Crafts architecture, such as dark wood moldings and lower ceilings. It is an architectural style that is "becoming"; a hybrid style that moves a house from one historical period to the next, blending elements of the old with the new. Perhaps at this time in my life that is why I found the house so magical, despite all the work that it would entail to restore and renew it. Perhaps I knew I had work to do on myself too; I will always be a work in progress.

Outside, in the back of my new/old house, tall, ancient pines line either side of the property. This makes me feel as if I am in a cathedral. Beyond is a marsh that we discover is filled with a chorus of spring peepers, small frogs that will let us know spring is here. There are the ghosts of flower and vegetable gardens behind the garage. While there is still a large amount of work to be done, I see all the ingredients of a garden. A garden that, despite years of neglect, under caring hands will bloom again.

I can never settle for accepting something just as it is. I'm compelled to find out "the history" of a person, place, or thing. I can't embrace or comprehend them fully unless I know where they come from, the path they traveled as they came to be in front of me. I spend many pleasant hours doing research online, at the library, or by reading books to come to this understanding. This tendency to uncover "the history" of something or someone made me a very good therapist. Perhaps there is some DNA involved; my grandmother had a library full of historical fiction and nonfiction. She always had a book about history on a table or tucked into a bag of knitting. My mother wanted to be a history teacher, though she never was. I did not know this until we were both much older, when she mentioned it as an afterthought. In college I majored first in history, later adding another major in sociology. My mentor and chair while completing my doctorate was a historian. These days I am researching the history of my new/old house. I want to know what influenced those who designed and built it. I wonder about what was occurring in the life of women then.

I find myself less interested in the Victorian influences on my house—the excess, the embellishments, the overwrought style of the period, the curio cabinets and rooms filled with "stuff." I am much more intrigued by the style my house was moving toward, initiated by the Arts and Crafts movement. The Arts and Crafts movement was a rebellion of sorts, which is probably why I am drawn to it. Its founders were some of the first critics of the Industrial Revolution. They were concerned about the race for progress, mass production, and the impact of industrialization on ways of working, the environment, and the human condition. They believed mechanized work alienates us from ourselves, and that things that are made should bring pleasure to the maker and the user. They advocated staying close to nature, finding joy in your work, creating objects that are beautiful and affordable to all, and living simply. As I read about the movement that influenced the architecture of my new/old house, what comes to mind is the famous line attributed to Mark Twain, "History doesn't repeat itself, but it often rhymes."

As I wait and watch this first year to see what's already been planted before I think about landscape and garden design, I research the history of gardens to imagine what mine might be.

I remember my grandmother's personal garden, the only one she tended herself. I am flooded with memories of the other gardens, the fruit trees, and the frogs that were also part of the landscape of my grandparents' home when I was a young child.

———————

My mother has descended another level down the steep staircase of dementia. These days it is uncertain whether she will know who I am, yet as the person I know fades and I try to come to grips with that reality, I remember who she was to me at different times in our lives. As chameleon-like as me, she shaped herself into the context of her life. She evolved with the arrival of every new child. She adapted to every undulation in my father's financial fortunes, and ultimately when he suffered a debilitating stroke at fifty-six. Because of the necessity she often faced to make more with less, my mother taught me the value of making the everyday, ordinary things in our lives interesting and beautiful. I remember the turquoise-and-orange jack-in-the-box costume she made me out of a cardboard box for Halloween. Perhaps it was from her I learned that the most mundane, inexpensive objects—like thrift store clothes, red lipstick, and sunglasses—can have magical properties.

When I am researching topics for my blog posts about What Nowness, I discover the term *everyday creativity*. It's used to describe the countless ways we are resourceful in our daily lives, ways that are often unrecognized and unrewarded and thus remain underdeveloped. We all have it, whether we express it by taking a different route to work, patching a moth hole in a sweater, or improvising that recipe we can't find. It need not be a traditionally creative activity, though it can be. We can see that every choice and decision we make throughout the day, regardless of how mundane they may seem, has a creative basis. You can teach yourself to appreciate and reimagine what you already have in your life, rather than say you don't have the talent or resources to begin a reinvention project or act on a deferred dream.

Being the oldest of all my siblings, I am the one who has traveled the longest with my mother. When I visit her, now more frequently because I am closer to where she lives, I sit on the arm of her chair and rub her back. I sing her favorite song, "Moon River." Now after many years, I call her Mommy again rather than Mom or Mother. Her head rests on my chest, and it is hard to tell whether I am comforting her or she is comforting me. Everything between us has always been unspoken and indirect. My ability to decode tells me we are comforting each other. We are both realists, and we know where this is headed. She can still remember some things but most of them are from her childhood and when she was a young woman. The events in her recent past are much harder to retrieve. My memory now, along with hers, also reaches with far greater clarity back to those moments when I was a little girl.

I am a child riding in our blue-and-white Ford. We make a turn onto the narrow road where my grandparents live. The damp, lush green darkness formed by the canopy of trees surrounds us and cools us down, a refuge from the hot concrete playground that adjoins our apartment building in the Bronx. There is a gate with a bell and a gravel driveway. We hop out of the car and ring it to announce our arrival. Hostas line a meandering bluestone walk, along with bursts of orange tiger lilies. Could this be the source of my delight, to find hostas already in place in my new/old house?

A farmhouse from the 1800s, my grandparents' home is set back from the road, and everything about it, both inside and out, references history. My grandmother chose Arts and Crafts–style furniture for every room. She covered beds with antique quilts. My grandfather's watercolors and pen-and-ink drawings from voyages to Europe years ago hang on the walls, evoking memories of the trips taken for their honeymoon and during the early years of their marriage. Everything in this house has a purpose, reflecting the hand of my pragmatic Dutch grandfather.

The kitchen table is against a window, and there is a *Peterson's Guide to Birds of the Northeast* sitting on the ledge for easy reference. Up the narrow stairs and to the left is a room that contains my grandfather's drafting table and a high stool. On the large screened-in porch, grown-ups have cocktails and children have Hires Root Beer and

Cheez Waffies, the only snack my grandfather ever served. It seemed an odd choice until my first trip to Amsterdam, where I found a waffle cookie—the Dutch stroopwafel—in our hotel room, and everywhere else we went, and suddenly understood my grandfather's enduring loyalty to a waffle.

Outside in the side yard are elaborate chairs my grandfather constructed from tree branches, a weathered gray. Way, way in the back of the property, my grandfather has set up a wading pool, its rounded edge painted yellow, with dancing green frogs. It attracts many real frogs, who sit on its wide brim as though it were a lily pad. Behind a nearby bush, my grandfather and I crouch, holding long blades of grass, and tickle their behinds until they jump in the pool with a splash. When we start school, we get a small patch of land somewhere on the property that becomes our very own garden. We can decide what to grow, and we have to tend to it when we come up for the weekend.

Our chores are garden-relevant: we help our grandmother pick a bouquet from her cut-flower garden to arrange in the vase on the long farmer's table in the dining room; we follow my grandfather, holding baskets, to pick vegetables for the meal. I experience my most happy and cherished childhood times here.

My grandfather died suddenly at sixty-three, and shortly afterward my grandmother sold this house and moved halfway across the country to live and travel with her two sisters. Rather than every weekend, as I had for my entire seven-year life, I now saw her maybe four times a year, and my grandfather no longer at all. My grandmother was the same age when she became a widow and embarked on a great adventure as I was when I started Accidental Icon.

My grandfather was converting the large barnlike garage into a dormitory to accommodate the growing numbers of his grandchildren when he died—a project, I one day discover, that future owners would complete as a guest house. The cooling balm of nature was gone from my life, replaced by the relentless heat and sun radiating from the concrete of the city. In this harsher environment, my mother lived without the support of her mother and grieved the death of her father. Here my father worked from early in the morning until after we were in bed at night. Here there was no longer nature to restore them.

In those precious years before my grandfather's death, my parents, my siblings, and I left each weekend spent at my grandparents' home rested and restored. Places that restore us, that occupy our attention by the opportunities they provide for play, exploration, curiosity, and rest, while important for me now that I am old, are important throughout our lifespan. It now becomes clear that everything I've done so far and imagined in my new/old house is in the service of re-creating this magical place where I spent some of the happiest moments of my life. I want my granddaughter to feel the same way about my new/old house too.

I'm attracted to all things old right now: houses, furniture, perennials, trees, and clothes. I'm looking at them in the hope they'll share some secrets they know about how to be old successfully. They all seem so satisfied with their circumstances, yet they still face the perils of severe weather, pests, moths, diseases, accidents, and other conditions that may shorten their lifespan or their ability to endure. We are determined to minimize buying new items for our house, instead finding recycled furniture, rugs, and period-correct light fixtures as we restore and furnish it. We've been doing a good job of it, except for one or two items like a comfortable organic mattress and new appliances. In all the old things we purchase for our new/old house, we see how attention and good care have allowed them to age so they remain beautiful and functional. Some of the things we buy have been skillfully repaired. I myself during this time learn how to repair a lamp. It's a tall brass one that we find on one of our trips to the many antique stores and flea markets that can be found in the Hudson Valley. I've been searching for a lamp that is just the right height to sit on the table between the two green velvet armchairs in front of the three bow windows in what used to be called a parlor. The tower room sits above. This lamp, tossed in a corner of the shop because of its need for repair, was quite a bargain. Between being frugal and fixing it myself, I feel very accomplished.

The marks or imperfections found on the used furniture we buy are evidence of a long and useful life, so they do not bother me. In our house, we find the prior owner used quick fixes that allow for a surface appeal but do not shore up or repair what lies below. Our dining room paneling, we later find, covers cracked plaster walls. There will be no quick fixes for us, nothing covered up. No matter how much you try to hide them, the markers of age will appear. We will use no artifice to try to make our house look new. Our mission here is to repair and restore in ways that respect the integrity of our new/old house. To enhance the beauty that comes from its age.

I reminisce about the early days of starting the blog. Because I had so fully accepted my age by the time I started it, I never imagined it to be a project about age. I saw Accidental Icon simply as a place to express my identity creatively through what I wore and my study of fashion. I now accept the idea that Accidental Icon was and is indeed a project about age. It dawns on me that it is a mission statement of sorts about how to be old.

Sometime during this past year, I've really accepted that I'm old and feel no shame, no despair about it. In fact, I decide to inhabit this new version of myself as completely as I do my house and the vintage clothes that hang upstairs in my "closet room." I decide to keep saying "I'm old" over and over until it drains all the pejorative connotations. I have learned to love being old by freeing myself from the grips of proclamations—like "60 is the new 40"—that still imply younger is better. This time it is me saying: This project is all about my age!

The way the media portrays it, there are two ways to be old. The first suggests you'll be frail, demented, lonely, invisible, and depressed. You'll be a drain on social programs and economic productivity, a caregiving burden to your family. You're most likely obese, no longer have sex, eschew technology, and are scorned by young people (#OKBoomer). You'll wear shapeless, baggy clothes and orthopedic shoes, stop using makeup, and have a permanent that gives you frizzy blue-tinged hair. You'll live in segregated communities with other old people, where you're parked like used cars until you die. At the end of the day, you're deemed pretty much worthless and disposable (à la the COVID-era hashtag #BoomerRemover). You are now a social problem. Who wants to aspire to any of those things? No wonder my fans in their twenties and thirties are terrified to be old.

The other way, expensive and not accessible to everyone, is to eat the right food, intermittently fast, and take a plethora of nutritional supplements to keep aging at bay. If you buy caviar serums (and devices with which to apply them) to use during a three-hour beauty routine, inject fillers, subject your body and brain to rigorous exercise, have sex all day long (varied positions recommended), and dye your hair, you'll keep looking young. If you move to the right place, use your life savings to become an entrepreneur, and work for the rest of your life doing something you love, you can live to be one hundred without growing old. Trying not to be old becomes your full-time job, and when you fail, you'll feel like crap. While you may be healthier if you do a few of these things, and some of that depends on your genetics, race, class, gender, ability, sexual orientation, and other demographics, you'll inevitably continue to look and grow old. Worst of all, you'll have no time to enjoy its pleasures, and you'll feel bad about yourself anyway. My fans who are in their sixties, soon to be seventies, like me, are looking for more meaningful ways to spend their time and money.

The first scenario implies that you can't control how you age, and the second insists that you can. What I have always known on some level is that neither one, by itself, reflects the lived reality or potential of our later life, and both cause young and older women alike to think that getting old is something to be avoided at all costs. What I have learned is that all you can control is the way you think about how to be old and respond creatively to the changes in your body as they happen. You can stay in the moment, or worry about what hasn't happened to you yet. You can accept stereotypes, or be the exception. You can be proactive about some things, but improvisational about others. There are events and happenings you can plan for prudently, and others will take you by surprise.

I'm reclaiming the word *old* because, as you know, I always believe we have the right to claim our own self-definition. I'm old, and I'm going to figure out how to be old and continue to tell my story.

Today, in my new/old house and life, I wear old denim jeans almost every day. I appreciate them as I never have before. Let's just say we completely understand each other. They seem to be the perfect fit. Will Accidental Icon survive the transition from city to country life? In these early days of exploring my new/old house, I don't have the answers yet, but I know with a great deal of certainty that no matter what, me and my denim jeans will be just fine. Even as we are fading and becoming more worn, we continue to create new narratives and add more value to ourselves with each passing day.

———————————

Somehow this new level of acceptance of my age allows me to finally finish the book proposal I have been unsuccessfully trying to write for the last three years. I'm taking a writing class, and one of the essays I submit will become the introduction to a book I have a new idea for. During this exploration, I find my form. It's loosely called a braided essay, one that incorporates both a personal story and research. It places my story in a greater context by writing about more than just me. These are essays that put meat on the bones of the blog writing I love. This form is the container that holds the two parts of me that have felt so disconnected: the creative and the academic, the art and the science. I feel whole in this kind of writing. When I look back at some of my earliest blog posts, I see they are more akin to the way I am writing now.

There is a community of writers that gathers on Zoom each day. Sessions occur four times a day, each in a different time zone. I write at 8:00 a.m. each day for fifty minutes in the company of hundreds of writers of every stripe from all over the world. We hold each other accountable to write while working silently together on Zoom. I count on them to help me not succumb to any self-imposed interruptions. Many mornings I'll keep writing after the session is over. I am determined to have a completed proposal by the end of the summer. I send the final version to my agent on August 1. The name I have chosen for this proposed book: *How to Be Old.*

As I write, I find my Instagram feed to be a great resource. It is like a little pocket diary that contains important events, dates, and photos of my life as Accidental Icon. During this year, 2021, I am still doing sponsored posts, but less frequently and more like the temp job I see it as. It is a means to an end. I save my money, make a budget, and plan that by the end of the year I will be done. I have a bridge to seventy, when I can collect my pension and Social Security. Calvin has found a way to take an early retirement. We will both be closing one door at the end of this year and opening a new one at the beginning of the next.

What I wear in my posts changes too. Early in the year I still wear clothes that brands like Dior lend me, sustainably designed clothes from emerging designers or vintage sent from shops. In the posts that are not sponsored, I stand in front of a full-length mirror in an empty room upstairs. Calvin is commuting, and I don't want him to use his weekends to take photos of me, so these are selfies taken from my phone.

They are as unretouched and unprofessional as the ones we took when I first began Accidental Icon. For this current improvisation, the wall is not white but celery green. In most of these photos I wear denim jeans. If you look closely, you can see some wires hanging and cracks in the wall. We've not yet gotten to the upstairs rooms. We are not quite done with our project of renovation and reinvention.

As the warmer weather comes, the photos move outdoors, portraits taken as I lean against the detached garage, sit in my garden, or walk a suburban street. Normally I would try to post at least three times a week. Now it's once if at all. The main reason I post at all is because of my followers. I always finish a post with a question, and I remain amazed at the seriousness and length in which it is answered. We are in a continuing conversation about so many topics: fashion, family, What Nowness, home, work, purpose, identity, older and younger life, reinvention, grief, loss, love, books, gardens, and any and all matters that concern the life of a woman. I am grateful for their company every day. Leaving Instagram would make me feel like I abandoned them. Even if I don't post for a couple of weeks, they never abandon me. No matter how infrequently the algorithms choose me to be seen, they always find me. They keep all the good parts of Accidental Icon alive. They are the good parts of social media.

I still feel a deep desire to use my hands differently than simply putting clothes made by others on my body. I want to engage with a garment more intimately through some act of creation, though I remain unsure what that act might be. I don't want to break up with my love of clothes; I just want to change my relationship with them. It will be something new/old, like my house. Like me. This new skill must include reuse. It needs to be something that also allows me to enjoy my love affair with nature, especially flowers. I post photos on Instagram of a yellow suit covered in flowers made from textile waste and sewn by a tailor somewhere in Africa. It stands in sharp relief against the green of the grass and trees behind me. Next to me on the ground is a pair of orange, feathered Prada slides I got some years back. I've taken them off. They are off to the side, like my old priorities. This suit is another designer's desire. Mine does not yet have a form, but vague outlines are taking place.

This week we approach the winter solstice. It is December, and last month we marked one year in our new/old house. In fact, today is the day before the solstice, the shortest day of the year. For many wild animals, the winter marks a time of dormancy and hibernation. It's a time when they are in complete harmony with the pace of their environment. I read in *Atmos* that they grow furrier coats, lower their body temperatures, and conserve metabolic energy. They productively use waste, breathe more slowly, and are very creative in how they spend their resources.

During the last six weeks I've gained weight, having slacked off on my yoga practice and the healthy routine I set for myself after being so ill last year. I have zero motivation to take photos of myself or post them. I don't want to engage in social media, and I can't make myself do it. After its pandemic hiatus, the fashion world has returned to normal, and even though I no longer live in the city, I still receive invitations to many events. I've declined most of them, preferring to remain at home and focus on tasks that make it more our own and more comfortable. I'm a social media person who does not want to be social. I've been very hard on myself about these behaviors. I don't like how I look. I won't even allow the grace of giving myself a break, despite the fact my mother is dying.

There are things that animals do in autumn to prepare for hibernation. Bears go through a time when they binge eat. This allows them to conserve energy during hibernation by providing stores of fat and protein. They also build, dig, or find a den. Essentially, they seek a safe space. For the female bear, during this hibernation time, in this space, she will give birth to and nurture her baby cubs. Even though the mating season occurs during the summer, the fertilized eggs will not begin development until hibernation begins.

Reading about these autumn behaviors in the natural world makes me less judgmental about my own preparation for what I know in my bones will be a dark winter as my mother journeys closer to her final days and dies. I feel too sad to go out, though the times I still post, I put on a brave face. I get the feeling I've lost things, but I'm unsure of what they are. I just know there are times I feel unexpectedly sad. Times

I feel there are things that have left my life but that I never got the chance to say goodbye to properly. These undefined losses are like piles of autumn leaves that will return to the earth and prepare the ground for something new. Yet right now they weigh me down and make me feel heavy. I move slowly, as if I am dragging the train of a very heavy dress.

While I most certainly will not be giving birth to another human, there is something else I need to conserve energy for: I am now contracted to labor and birth a book. The week after my agent sold the book and I signed the contract, my mother began to spend all of her time sleeping. It's almost as though she felt her work was done and she could rest.

There is the need to prepare a space that is mine, to free myself from the distraction of social media so I can lean in, to have plenty of internal resources to draw upon, to remember the past but allow room for the future. I must have room to grieve. These are all things that are necessary to support the process of reflection and writing necessary to produce a book that is a memoir. My behaviors this autumn makes sense when placed in this frame. I am so much kinder to myself with this realization. I look in the mirror and see myself as I really am. I'm okay.

———————

On my front lawn, in front of a bay of windows and to the right of my beautiful blue hydrangeas, are two high director's chairs, screens, lights, and cameras. There is a truck parked out front. My neighbors wonder what's going on. In what is perhaps my last official act as a public badass, I'm going to be interviewed by CNBC.

Recently there has been a public fascination with old people who appear on Instagram and TikTok. This time the headlines read "Senior Influencers, or 'Graninfluencers,' Are Smashing Stereotypes and Making Big Bucks as Social Media Sensations." I am featured as an example in all the pieces with other old folks with whom I have nothing in common except for gray hair. These headlines do not tell my authentic story. I take great offense, because while they allege we are breaking stereotypes, they are using stereotypes to describe us. If you google "ageist language," you will find the words *senior* and the phrase *calling someone grandma*. Both rank high on the list.

The process of self-definition, which can only come when we have self-understanding, becomes urgent as we get older because we encounter forces that seek to make us invisible, suggest we are no longer useful or beautiful, and write a different story about us than the one we may wish to write for ourselves. We must know who we are and be strong enough to meet the forces that seek to constrain us.

I am contacted by all the major news stations and by shows like *Entertainment Tonight* and *Access Hollywood* to talk about how great it is to be an "instagramma." I agree with one condition: that I be able to address how ageist the language and description of who we are and what we do is. How it strips us of our uniqueness and individual stories. The only outlet that takes me up on my offer is CNBC. That's why they're here filming on my front lawn, and I can't wait to have my say. So yes, no matter what else changes, I will always be a badass when I need to be.

Calvin and I set out in the car, taking the back roads rather than the highway. Following the river, we pass through small cities and towns in various stages of development. Some, like mine, once abandoned or left in disrepair, now show signs of life, propagated by the many transplants from Brooklyn and other boroughs. Thanks to the entrepreneurial spirit of the city folk who have moved here, there are new businesses, online and brick-and-mortar. Because of them and the community of creatives they are engaging, we will have a maker's holiday market this year. Our new/old car has heated leather seats that keep me warm. Slow jazz repetitions accompany us when we take this journey, lulling me into a tenuous sense of security. At the end of the drive is my mother.

She is now in the last stages of dying. Unlike the usual brisk, taking-care-of-business approach to her life, she's taking her time with her death. Each week she does less. She rarely speaks, no longer eats, and takes only sips of fluid. Now, rather than staying busy with reading, doing her crosswords, and praying novenas for her children (and anyone else who needs them), she sleeps. The crystal rosary I brought her from a cathedral in Strasbourg three years ago no longer sends out sparks of light as her fingers animate it, moving along the beads. There are no more murmured Hail Marys, only sorrowful, mournful silence.

As I tidy up her room, I come upon a woven china basket she's had for as long as I can remember. It's one of the few possessions that has moved with her to all the places she's lived in. In the past it contained all her prayer cards, novenas, and rosaries. It came with her to this place when she arrived six years ago. Now she fills it with Mass cards for those who have taken this path before her: her sisters, their husbands, her parents, her friends, her nephews, and my father. Her card will complete the pile. My stomach contracts with the knowledge that my generation comes next. Hospice began this week. I do not know yet that she will die on Christmas morning. Or that in the week before my mother dies, after she visits her grandmother for the last time, my daughter, after trying for seven years for a second child, will become pregnant with my grandson. She announces the pregnancy by producing a sonogram and saying, "Grammy left us a little surprise."

Two generations behind me, and three generations behind my mother, my granddaughter remains exempt from this waiting for death. She is full of only one thing right now: the incredible excitement that children enjoy at Christmas. She reminds me urgently that I must get a tree this year, put up decorations, and find pride of place for the two tiny gingerbread houses she made and decorated with brightly colored candy. Instead of slow jazz, she wants me to play Christmas music, as loud and celebratory as the volume controls allow. She tells me I must be ready because Santa will come to my house too. Last year I got away with opting out of decorating because I had just moved, but this year, with a determination reminiscent of my mother's, it's clear she will tolerate no excuse.

There are cookies to bake for the neighbors who brought us plants when we arrived and left vegetables from their gardens during the summer and apple turnovers when it was apple-picking time this fall. It's my turn to return their neighborly hospitality and acknowledge the gifts that were given, small kindnesses that eased the adjustment to our new community and home. It would be easy for me to evade these responsibilities by simply explaining I am too busy standing guard over my mother in her final days, but it would disappoint her if I offered that as an excuse. After all, she remained present, living, and loving as she experienced the death of all those she loved. After my father died, she allowed herself to become our greatest comfort.

We buy a Christmas tree, a live one, in a big red tub. This Christmas it can stay in the house because it is small, but in the New Year we will plant it outside because it will grow tall. In crafting our decorations, we choose a theme of life and rebirth. I have cranberries to string, pine cones gathered from under our towering white pines, evergreen and boxwood garlands to weave between the spokes of our staircases, inside and out. All these materials will return as compost to the earth, where they will reconstitute and regenerate, providing rich soil for future growth. The smell of

Christmas comes into my house, and from this I experience bursts of joy amid the sadness.

After our trips to visit my mother, we make stops at thrift and vintage stores, looking for ornaments that have lived a life on other people's trees. I sift through baskets of them like I'm on a treasure hunt. Now they are given second life on our tree, and someday I hope they will be packed up and given to my granddaughter for her own tree, in her own home.

I hang foil-covered balls of chocolate ornaments that will disappear as they are plucked and eaten. I search for a cookie recipe that is festive but not too difficult; my kitchen is, like me, in the process of renovation. I decide on a rich, soft chocolate cookie topped with shards of crumbled candy canes. Everything triggers a memory of my mother these days, and I remember that chocolate mint is one of her favorite flavors. In my mind I see the long, narrow boxes of chocolate dinner mints she bought for holiday tables. I can almost taste the refreshing jolt of the mint, waking me up and reminding me that I am alive. Even as she aged, her favorite treat remained York Peppermint Patties, and we, all her children, brought her bags of them. No matter how many we brought, they always disappeared before the next visit.

My mother and my granddaughter, wiser than me, are teaching me how to continue living life when in the company of death. My Christmas tree tells me that life goes on.

We will continue to grow and strengthen each year. My ornaments say, *There will be a new purpose for you when this time is over, though some familiar and loved things will disappear.* The evergreens and boxwoods reveal that nature allows us to reconstitute and become something new; to nurture those who come behind us. While one life ends, others go on, and for those, we must remain present. It's the nature of things, they both tell me; life goes on.

69

Let the Old Become New Again

t's Sunday morning. Sleeping in for me is now to seven thirty, since during the week I am up at five to do some writing before my grandson arrives at six. Calvin is already up, and I can smell the freshly ground, freshly brewed coffee. I enter my new/old kitchen with its cheery buttercup-yellow cupboards. Light streaks across the golden heart-pine floor. The room glows. My hand curls around the green ceramic mug that holds my coffee. It's the same color as the walls. Warmth flows through my palm. The color of this week's $3.99 Trader Joe's bouquet catches my eye, a small treat that brings pleasure all week long during the winter. In the summer, flowers come from my garden.

I've often wanted to have regular deliveries of flowers to my house, as I love the sight and smell of them. The cost in the scheme of other obligations was prohibitive. Until my own garden blooms, I've satisfied my desire within the constraints of a now more limited income. Trader Joe's gets fresh flower deliveries seven days a week. And they last longer than the more expensive bouquets I received from brands on my birthday or to mark a lucrative partnership. Each small bunch of blooms conveys a subtle color scheme. This week I chose orange. There are calla lilies and gerbera daisies, intermingled with splashes of purple and magenta from supporting players.

The light and warmth I find in my kitchen seep into my pores. I am excited. Today we are going to explore a new small town in the Hudson Valley. I think about what I will wear, and now, what Calvin will wear too. Calvin and I recently accepted a proposal that we model as a couple. We met my former modeling agent for dinner when she was in New York, and she pitched the idea. I began this year with no other agent, save my literary one. I was very hesitant about this new modeling proposition. I first said yes, then said no. I worried I might lose myself again. I like not having to answer to anybody. I no longer have to conform to someone else's schedule, check things out before I decide to take something on, or wear what a brand or creative director wants me to wear. But Calvin seemed to want to try it. This time I support him in this creative exploration because when I wanted the same thing he supported me. We negotiate for terms that say we will only work as a couple. We will not do "influencing" work or sponsored posts. Our house, our grandchildren, and my writing take priority. We will only do maybe three or four jobs a year, which our new/old agent promises to make worth our while.

In a role reversal, this time I will be the one taking photographs of the place we are heading to. I am the one in control of the camera's aperture and f-stops. A self-timer allows me to jump into the shot. Together, both equally visible, we embark on a new reinvention. Our destination today is twenty-six minutes from where we live, a drive through some mountains and across a bridge to the other side of the river. We do not know what we will find when we get there, except for a coffeehouse we saw on Instagram that suggests there might be some interesting places and people there. I take a video of Calvin driving with my phone. He looks happy. I am happy.

Calvin and I met at a bookbinding workshop twenty-five years ago. The workshop happened every Sunday afternoon in the basement of a building in the East Village home of the Asian American Writers' Workshop. Books written by Asian American writers and copies of the zine *Bamboo Girl* filled the bookcases. In the center of the room were three large round tables for us to work on. We shared our writing, our thoughts, and the books that sprang from our hands. In my bag from Pearl Paint was linen thread, PVA glue, needles, beeswax, an awl for punching holes, and a smooth ivory bone folder. Our teacher, a book artist from Nova Scotia, provided the binding board. I haunted paper stores to find material that was just right for the project I envisioned.

I met Calvin at a place and time where I was doing a good amount of writing and creating a new version of a self. I was recently divorced and had been living in New York City for four years. My daughter spent weekends with her father. For the first time since I was a kid, my weekends were free of work and for me, only me. While I did some dating during that time, I spent those four years of weekends mostly taking writing classes, going out Latin dancing with a younger friend, and doing the work on myself that I didn't do, and should have, before I got married. When I did date, it was usually someone who was a creative of some sort, a musician or photographer. Calvin worked in a physics lab. He is a nerd like me. My attitude by the time I took the workshop was, if I meet someone, that's nice, but if I don't, I'm perfectly fine with being alone. I imagine that if I were single today at age sixty-nine, I would try my hand at a dating app, or find people to reach out to on Instagram, as I do now to find friends. I have discovered that many older people find dates these ways.

From the beginning, Calvin and I did not try to define what we were doing together. In our uniquely individual ways, we both resist categorization. We are friends, passionate about exploring the potential in ourselves as creative people and, for Calvin, as an Asian man who was raised by German foster parents on Long Island, about reclaiming his cultural identity. Calvin is not the name he was given at birth, but one he received from his foster family. Even after he had connected with his identity as an Asian man, he kept the name because he loved his foster family, and they had given it to him.

When Calvin was not performing in the Asian American improv group Peeling the Banana and I was not working on my installation, we went to art exhibitions, plays, and festivals together. Puzzled by the undefined nature of our relationship, friends would ask each of us privately, "Are you dating?" We would shrug our shoulders and say nothing; what we experienced with each other was something the word *dating* did not contain. It was about identity, healing, and discovering who we were becoming in the company of another whose soft, undemanding touch allowed us to do so.

Today we are still resisting a definition of who we are together. After twenty-five years of partnership, we are living together but not married. We are not alone in this decision, as there has been an enormous increase in cohabitating among people our age. We revisit the question at certain times when it becomes relevant, like now, when we are navigating pensions and Social Security. We've invested in legal documents—wills, trusts, power of attorney, health care proxy—that protect us, since we are not legally married and domestic partner laws have a limited scope. For us, the pros-and-cons list still comes out to stay as we are. We keep separate finances, separate interests, and separate selves. That is, until recently, when we bought a house and signed a modeling contract together.

We do not feel slighted or ignored if we become unavailable to each other because of immersion in our singular pursuits. We tolerate the messes we both create while doing so. Revealing our age, we revel in the idea that we are "shacking up." I guess this is not too surprising; it was our generation that made cohabitation an option. Again, we shrug when asked—and it happens more often than we like—"Will you two ever get married?" We feel that the richly colored threads we each bring from our lives are more beautifully entwined in this arrangement than they could ever be in a formal marriage. And we both know from personal experience that legal bonds are hard as hell, and costly to get out of. If you idealized marriage before a divorce, you certainly become more realistic afterward.

When I first started Accidental Icon, Calvin was a silent partner. He could wear whatever he wanted behind the camera. Now I am the stylist for us both. During our forays as urban nomads, we attracted people curious about who we were and what we were doing. We made friends and connections and had plenty of stimulating conversations. We've had coffee with many young artists, like us trying to express their creative selves. Social media was a democratizing hand up for us and them. It was free exposure.

Once we got our photo on those trips out onto the streets of New York, it would be time to find a place we'd never been to before for coffee or brunch. We'd stumble into bookstore cafés furnished with comfortable purple velvet vintage couches, lofts with distilling equipment for small-batch whiskey, and tea shops with menus five pages long. There was a new idea, a vision, an inspiration, and something never seen or imagined that would find its way into a photo or a blog post. We would head home on the subway. We were that kind of tired that is extremely pleasant. We were full. At the end of these days, we felt rich, even though we weren't making much money then.

My Instagram grid is a visual record of Accidental Icon from the first post in 2014 to the one I am planning to post this week, in 2023. I can trace all the pivot points, changes in direction. I am flooded with memories of how much fun it was to be her. The year or two she lost her way is just a blip on the screen. It just matters that I am who I am today. Now I am headed in a new direction, telling a different story. The part of me that is Accidental Icon is not gone. I've just reinvented her again, exactly the way I did in 2014. I've recycled and reused the pieces of Accidental Icon that still serve my growth and my dreams. Because of this epiphany, this new level of self-acceptance, this forgiveness of mistakes made, this Sunday, for the first time since we agreed to do this modeling thing, I feel cautiously optimistic. I envision the photos and what we will wear. Like before, we do not know what we will find when we arrive in this little town we have never been to. We'll walk up and down the streets like we once did in New York. It's a crisp winter's day.

I decide the hero piece for us both will be oversize vintage coats. Calvin wears a black wool Comme des Garçons overcoat. I gifted it to him because while I just loved the cut, even for me it was too oversize. Patagonia winter fleece pants and trail hiking sneakers, along with a tailored brown Barbour shirt, complete the look for him. I wear a black wool oversize Dior men's coat that required some minimal tailoring. I have discovered a skilled tailor near our new/old house; being five foot two, I find myself in frequent need of someone who can sew a hem. I take off my Birks for a minute, substitute some lug-sole boots, and pair them with vintage Dior jeans. I wear a black Margaret Howell roll-neck boiled wool sweater.

I try a pair of my big hoop signature earrings. In this reinvention, they just don't seem to work for me the way they did before. I decide to keep on the small silver huggies I've been wearing. Except for my boots, everything I wear is from a resale site or a flea market. We put on our respective black sunglasses, grab my camera and tripod, and hit the road. Sunglasses will always be a part of my public story. There will always be a part of me never revealed.

Calvin and I now spend most of our time together. He still has his bike friends and photography meetups, and I have my own pursuits, but since he retired early from his full-time job and I am no longer gallivanting all over the world as Accidental Icon, we are more often together than not. I find we can't keep our hands off each other, like when we first met, but it's a different way of coming together. Whenever we pass each other in the house, there is a touch on the shoulder, a kiss on the forehead or sometimes on the lips. We often stop what we are doing to give each other a long hug, and I tuck my head under his chin and feel the constancy of his beating heart. We hold hands when we walk to the store. This kind of touching is slow and delicious, as if we have all the time in the world. The primary energy fueling our touch these days is love and gratitude—for each other, and for the life we have created since becoming partners. The sexual aspect, while still there, has become less intense over time, less spontaneous and harder to accomplish without some effort. However, the reward is a feeling of satisfaction that differs from before; now we take our time. Quality has become more important than quantity.

We recently purchased twin vintage lounge chairs, which we set next to each other in our backyard. When we are in them, we reach over to hold each other's hand. We joke that the two chairs are our version of the Viagra bathtub commercial. Our fantasy entails rolling off the chairs onto the lush green lawn and stripping naked. Even better if there is a soft spring rain to caress our entwined bodies as we do the same to each other for an entire lazy afternoon. I imagine grass stains on my butt. Perhaps one day we will be moved to enact our fantasy of having sex in the great outdoors, as we did the year we first met, bodies freely loving at any age. In the meantime, because our proximate neighbor makes use of surveillance cameras to protect his property, what we do with each other happens in our new bed, with its comfortable sustainable mattress and antique quilt. I must admit, though, that we sometimes feel it would be worth the risk as we imagine the look on our neighbors' faces.

Our ride to a new Hudson River town this Sunday is full of anticipation, and Calvin looks handsome as he drives. We are a couple that wear pre-owned clothes and ride in a pre-owned car. We find that we need a car in this new life outside New York City. Calvin sets his mind to find us the very best of a used one, and he does—luxurious and looking brand-new on the outside, with working parts and interior that have been treated with care. Calvin believes the longevity of the car working at top performance is worth our investment. He's taken on the project of extending its life, and his commitment is clear in how he maintains it. Our new/old car makes me think much more about what living a long life means. I measure longevity not in actual years but in how long, with attentive servicing, something or someone can function optimally.

There's so much we know about what things we can do throughout our now extended lifespan to age beautifully, remaining functional and vibrant for a long time, just like my car and the pieces that have entered my new/old home. I've been digging into the research and identifying practices and activities that I can incorporate into daily living that will support my desire to love, work, and live the fullest and best life I can as I'm heading up the hill to seventy. It's pretty simple: get enough sleep, minimize stress, eat a plant-based diet, and exercise regularly, both cardio and strength. Interestingly, I find experts say these practices can and should begin while we're young. The best part, though, is that it's never too late to start.

On the beautiful Sunday morning of our Hudson Valley trip, we arrive at our destination and find the main street populated by yoga studios, taverns, restaurants, general stores, and the coffee shop that enticed us here to begin with. My Leica hangs from my neck, and Calvin carries the tripod. We cross the street, ready for a coffee. I'm struck immediately by the coffee machines. I later discover they are called lever machines, made in Italy. Expert artisans hammered the texture by hand into the silver surface, embellished with copper accents. The machines are a work of art, producing exquisite espresso.

Open to all possibilities today, I ask the barista to recommend something. The bite of espresso amid the sweet pistachio surprises my tongue. I take photos of the objects, the light, the lever machines. A couple with two children approaches, and we chat. When told our story of being recent NYC transplants, they reveal seeing us get out of the car. They thought we were artists of some sort and lived in the city. Our clothing and the camera around my neck revealed our identity. They are a younger version of us, from another time. They live in Queens, and met while attending the School of Visual Arts. The wife is a designer; the husband is a painter. Both, of course, with day jobs, as we always had. We reminisce about New York City over the decades we lived there. We exchange information, get invited to a gallery opening on the Lower East Side. We invite them to Peekskill. Another time, a different place, a familiar conversation.

We venture out, looking for a scene to shoot our couple portrait for the week. I spot a brick building, a terra-cotta wall, different shades of color, different textures, a boarded-up window, a pile of leaves to stand in, combining to create the soft, dark moodiness I seem to favor in my photos. Calvin's used to have a sharper edge; mine are softer. I set the timer for twelve seconds and jump into the shot. I'm happy with the work. We're ready to find a place we've never been to before for lunch. We do, a small café with interesting names for sandwiches, like Moon River and The Dream. An employee hand-writes the menu on pieces from a cardboard box.

Back in our new/old car, our new/old selves feel that spark again—the excitement of new beginnings. We are full. We decide to take a risk: no GPS on the way home. We figure we'll find our way, since we have a sense of the general direction we need to go in. We know that if we get lost, we can always get found again. My photos are the same but different from those Calvin took in 2014. We review them together in our new/old kitchen, as we did before at the counter in our old place in East Harlem. Different time, different place, familiar conversation.

During the period when my house was built, the early 1900s, the zeitgeist included a deep yearning for a more stable time, a return to native plants and a turn away from professionally designed gardens. I read about and discover "grandmother's gardens." I see vestiges of a grandmother's garden in the meandering, overgrown plantings in our yard; the ghosts of their harvest linger under the porch in a cellar formerly used for canning and drying herbs. Faded labels on the shelves reveal what was stored here years ago.

Shortly before and during the time my house was built, women encouraged one another to garden as a release from the constraints of the lives they lived indoors as caregivers and women. Women's suffrage was happening, and women were moving out of the house and into the world. Grandmother's gardens became transitional spaces where they could discover their own voices and create their own identities. Many women who created these informal yet colorful and exuberant gardens went on to successful careers as garden writers, painters, and photographers. They used their gardens to reinvent themselves as artists. Grandmother's gardens became an outlet for physical activity and creativity. Organized around everyday activities, they contained a mash-up of vegetables, herbs, and flowers. There was a return to heirloom plants with a long history in gardens; irises, peonies, daffodils, snowdrops. I discover these flowers in random patches scattered throughout my side and back yard. We have transplanted them into beds that are more intentional, yet in a way that blends into the landscape, as if nature was the one who planted them there. Around our patio, framed by a pergola patiently and expertly constructed by Calvin, I grow an assortment of herbs, roses, lavender, lettuce, beans, and boxwoods.

I love that grandmother's gardens were places where women could create, maintain their health, and enjoy a reprieve from their role as constant caregivers. They offered a connection between family and the country's past in a way that enriched, rather than substituting for or evading, the present. The women who wrote about, designed, and photographed these gardens were reinventing themselves just as some of us have been doing during this time of older life as we discover, refind, and set free the people we were always meant to be during our lifetimes.

Grandmother's gardens put me in mind of my grandmother, the one who I never met, who died at a very young age. I wonder what kind of grandmother she would have been. I think of my other grandmother, the one who ran away. Now that I live so close to my grandchildren, I am figuring out what kind of grandmother I am going to be. I always admired my runaway grandmother for being such a rebel, for doing something most women of her time did not dare to do. I wonder whether, if my grandmother had taken up her cello again after my grandfather died, if it might have given her life the meaning she sought through her acquisition of novel things and experiences. Perhaps her music had meant so much to her that she could not bear to have it abruptly taken away again. Perhaps losing her home meant that she would never attach to a house again. As I write these words, I realize that my new/old house is my way of returning to the place that was so abruptly taken from me. For the first time, I feel a flash of anger toward my grandmother. I always thought my mother was unjust to be so angry at her. Perhaps I can now see why.

My daughter tells me she could not imagine how she would manage my grandchildren, a long commute, and a demanding job if I was not close by. Yet I also understand why my grandmother may have returned to the comfort of her sisters and the life she had years before, when she had a purpose, when she was an artist. For my grandmother and to her children, it was clear over the years that being a mother and grandmother did not provide her with a purpose she wished to invest in. Or maybe when she and my grandfather lost everything during the Depression and my grandfather later left the world so abruptly, it became too risky to commit to anything or anyone except herself. Perhaps she wanted to be someone who was not a mother or grandmother, who enjoyed traveling and was not satisfied with a woman's life as it was prescribed for her during the time she lived. But as my mother taught me, not everything needs to be either/or.

The sky is blue; the sun is high in the sky. It is one of those days that is neither too cool nor too hot. It's perfection. I am delighted to have the company of my eight-year-old granddaughter; she has a day off from school, but her parents are working. Sprawled on an old quilt, crimson with outlines of black and white chrysanthemums, we are sitting in the middle of the great expanse that is our back lawn. My granddaughter calls me Coco. My daughter suggested this nickname to her as an alternative to "Grandma" because of my association as Accidental Icon with the world of fashion, and because a traditional grandmother name was not a good fit for her nontraditional mother. Perhaps my daughter was not yet ready to see me as someone who is old. The word *grandma* is used to signal a woman is old. Yet I know women in their forties, not much older than my daughter herself, who are grandmothers. That's the problem with stereotypes: they simplify what is always a much more complex phenomenon. In any case, "Coco" is easy for a toddler to say, and has become synonymous with "grandmother" in my family. My granddaughter asks all her little friends if they have a Coco too.

Joining us on the quilt is a picnic lunch, bunches of wildflowers we have collected from the edges of my property, and a large leather antique photo album with a latch. My new grandson is sleeping beside us. Until he is an older baby, because I am no longer an Accidental Icon, childcare for this little one is full time; 6:00 a.m. to 4:00 p.m., Monday through Friday. Not all of us are grandparents, some by choice and others not, so I try to not talk about my grandchildren incessantly.

Grandmother is just one of the many roles I occupy; the more roles and, as I like to say, selves we have, the greater our ability to relate to many people of all ages, enriching our lives in countless ways. This is another reason I object to the moniker "instagramma." It makes me, as Accidental Icon, into a stereotype. It erases all the other parts of me, denies my complexity, as if my age is the only interesting thing about me. I am so much more than just a grandma. But that is an important part of me too. Just as when I was a mom, there are other parts of my identity that have held importance for me and new identities that I still aspire to. And yet in motherhood, and now in grandmotherhood, it is a struggle not to lose those other mes. Trying to not lose them becomes an important part of staying in balance. Our roles are fluid and change throughout our lives. Mothers, lovers, married or not, workers, professionals, caregivers, retired, or unemployed, sometimes it's hard to remember that who we are inside is someone who transcends roles, even though it may be hard to find her when the roles she plays become all-consuming. Perhaps that is what happened to my grandmother. She was trying to refind who she had been. It seems in older life we get the gift of rediscovering the person we may have lost as our roles changed. In older life, I have found I contain identities I've never known before. At any age, we can become someone we never knew before.

I always knew I would enjoy being a grandmother, but I could never have predicted how completely besotted I am with this little girl, and now this little boy. I also did not know that as an older person, hugs from this delightful girl and keeping this newborn close in a soft gray baby carrier could strengthen my immune system, lower my blood pressure, protect me from depression, and reduce my levels of stress. I also learn that our relationship is a benefit for them too; a good relationship with a grandparent increases a child's feelings of well-being.

My granddaughter's imagination knows no bounds. She is the author of countless adventures that I receive her patient instruction on how to act out. She wants to be a spy and knows all about the CIA, so us being spies having to save the world or get out of danger is a frequent theme. Her intuition astounds me; it feels like we are in some kind of peril right now. Whether that be the devastating effects of climate change, school shootings, or losing democracy, danger and a need for salvation are certainly in the air. She is like the canary in the coal mine. I've made sure she knows that from 2018 to 2021, the director of the CIA was a woman.

She is a lover of nature and takes great delight in the outdoor spaces we have created: the grandmother's garden, the huge Japanese maple in our front yard where she can sit in the crook of a branch and observe the neighborhood. Her favorite spot is on the slope in the back, where Calvin has fashioned her a "secret hideout" underneath bending tree branches and overgrown vines. He's built some stairs to reach it and a bench inside that accommodates a long cushion where we sit and she tells me all her secrets and her wonderful imaginings. It is where we retreat to when we are in danger as spies. We can take a nap there. She's helped to create these places. After endless walks in our local nursery and much contemplation, she has chosen plants and flowers that now occupy pride of place in the garden. She's planted seeds in the ground that later become what makes a delicious supper salad, and she's carefully picked roses to place in the bud vases we've collected from flea markets.

She tells me how much she loves me often, says thank you all the time. The trait that we share is our anger toward things we perceive as unjust, and together we have written advocacy letters for changes in rules she believes are unfair; interestingly, they usually have something to do with the arbitrariness of chronological age or required height for getting admitted to amusement park rides, as she is small for her age.

Today our task is to press some wildflowers in the antique book, and I am amazed at the innovative ways she takes the flowers apart to make collages of color. This child is never just literal. In her mind, ordinary things become magical. I suppose this is another way we are alike. We have some blossoms left over, and I get the idea to make us flower crowns. I show her how to make a slit with your nail in the stem and how to slide one flower into another. The crowns we are making today are full of yellow buttercups and the violets that grow wild across our lawn. We both wear one, and we take each other's photo. Then we get up and dance together in the yard, as we have now magically become fairies.

Time rolls back, and I am eight years old too. I can't remember who taught me how to make flower crowns when I was a girl, but I want her to remember, when she is soon to be seventy, that it was her grandmother. I think there is a better chance now that she will, because I have become a different grandmother than the ones I had; different from the one who died before I was born and never knew, different from the one who left me behind for new clothes and traveling the world. The grandmother I almost was.

Once again, I am struck by how different and individual the aging journey is. The number of resources we have access to, our social position, our health or lack thereof, geography, family relationships, and the losses we have experienced all shape the journey. Statistically, women live longer than men, so chances are they may at some point find themselves alone. Women are cohabitating without the benefit of marriage, as I am. Women are in committed relationships yet keep their own living space. Many older women are experimenting with breaking the rules, just like my granddaughter is. Friends are jointly buying property so they may retire together. Older women are opening up their homes to students for help with household chores, forging mutually caring relationships. We are becoming online-dating people, starting-our-own-business people. We care for parents and support children and grandchildren, all at the same time. We are a multitude of women reinventing, adapting, and finding our way. It reminds me of being young and badass in the 1970s, reinventing roles for women about sexuality, work, and parenting. Our time for revolution has come around again; we did a lot of rebelling in the 1970s. How ironic is it that as many women from my generation approach our seventieth birthday, we are once again reinventing our lives, roles, and opportunities? The seventies seem to be the magic number for badass women doing it differently, for sure.

Today the statue of the Blessed Mother sits in a back corner, under a shady tree. There is a white antique iron and fili-greed bench, found at a flea market. This is the place where I sit when I need to feel and find my mother, to share with her all the epiphanies the last year of her life and death have brought me. I miss her. I feel closer to her here in nature than anywhere else.

My granddaughter picks bright blue asters for the vase on my dining room table. They are the color of my mother's eyes and the faded denim I now wear every day. I make up a song about frogs sitting on lily pads, eating flies, and sing it to my grandson. I have a silver spoon next to my plate and fully intend for them both to have manners. I will teach them to be thoughtful of others and of the earth. I've been getting Arts and Crafts furniture. Some of Calvin's photo-graphs hang on our walls.

In my renovated kitchen there are bright yellow cabinets, an Arts and Crafts design, but with modern appliances. A bottle warmer and bottles are on the counter. It is here, in the heart of my home, that I write this book. My writing room upstairs is too far from where I find inspiration for this story, too isolated. Here, creative expression, an artistic self, partnering, mothering, and grandmothering can coexist. I am grateful for all the choices I have that my two grandmothers and my mother did not. Mine are not absolute, nor are they either/or as theirs seemed to be.

Today I am getting dressed to go pumpkin picking with my granddaughter, grandson, daughter, son-in-law, and Calvin. It's cool and overcast, so I'm happy to wear a light gray, oversize, sustainably made sweater I recently received as a gift—the first I have not declined in a long time. What I like about it is that any woman, playing any role, could wear it. I add the softest suede loafers with a tassel, also light gray, a reminder of one of the last shoots I did before life got interrupted. I wear my oldest pair of jeans, which still fit comfortably. I got them before I was an Accidental Icon. Today my jeans are worn and feel as light as the exquisite suede loafers that make it seem I am wearing a slipper rather than a shoe. I splattered my jeans with white paint that matches the rafters under my garage roof, which I painstakingly painted last year. They make me feel accomplished. I could be mistaken for an artist.

I add a pair of Céline reading glasses. I had them made from a frame I got on a resale site where I have been selling clothes I wore as an Accidental Icon that no longer suit me. My lambskin fanny pack, courtesy of agnès b., allows for holding a fussy baby or easily chasing an eight-year-old who is always determined to color outside the lines and go off the beaten path. A Do Not Enter sign always holds a mysterious allure for her. Wonder who she resembles? As I look at the outfit I chose today, I think that any woman at any age could wear it on a blustery fall day to the local pumpkin patch.

Today I head back to the city. I discover there are certain things I can only find there. While I love my new home on the Hudson, some experiences of my former life are just irreplaceable. This includes having a haircut with my Japanese hairstylist Jun. I've tried a few stylists up here, but they just don't seem to know how to handle my stubborn thick, straight hair. My hair resists them. Another is a bagel shop close to the salon. A trip to Jun always involves a bagel and coffee. Today is no different.

I decide to walk up Madison Avenue on my way to the salon. Tucked away on an inconspicuous block, it's called Tokuyama. A Japanese lantern hangs outside the door. I've prepared for this day by acquiring new sunglasses. This pair is not from a classic fashion house like Chanel but from a small independent designer. Nearsighted, the designer always struggled to find glasses, and determined she would one day design her own. Her forte is shape and color. The glasses play with lines and circles. They are quirky and cool. Her website description says the glasses I chose are "like raising a fist in an elegant way." I imagine they will be the perfect accessory for what will be my new haircut. I ordered mine in black. I'm contemplating going for the orange ones too.

As I walk past flagship stores, memories flash. There is the time I visited Carolina Herrera's atelier. Soon after, I wore a camel coat with cascading embroidered flowers to her show. Inside Marc Jacobs, I huddled on the top floor, looking down with other influencer friends years younger than me at the riotously colorful show of the Japanese designer Tomo Koizumi. A variety of influences inspires his ruffled tulle creations, including Japanese dolls and flower sculptures. I pass the new Hermès location and remember a trip to Paris and a new bag. It sits in its orange box, waiting for my next adventure. I see boots I covet at Loro Piana. They are the same color and butter-soft suede as the loafers I received to do a post where I dressed in the brand. I pass Anne et Valentin, where I found my most interesting glasses, the best prescription glass. Now, after cataract surgery, I no longer require prescriptions, a silver-lining perk that comes from being old.

Every time I've done something to my hair, there've been emotional implications: stretching, excitement, desire, urgency, anxiety, pressure, rebellion, force, anger, yearning. I've often changed my hairstyle in order to mark an event in my life, to signify a new passage, to defy expectations, to subvert the old and make room for the new. There are social stories and scripts about hair, femininity, and culture that I've used to my rebellious advantage. My hair has always been a statement about self and society.

When I was a child, someone other than myself controlled my hairstyle. My mother preferred to cut it quite short, like a boy's. In most childhood pictures, I'm sporting a pixie cut like Twiggy's before she even came onto the scene. Once I was old enough to control my hair narrative, I wore it long, not because that is what all the girls did but because it was rebellious. I parted it in the middle and it was bone straight.

Long hair in the 1970s was associated with counterculture figures like Grace Slick and Jim Morrison. Long hair was psychedelic rock, getting high, and breaking the rules that strict parents and Catholic school had imposed. Long hair was political. In high school, the times and spaces my body could move in, what I could wear, what was acceptable to express, were all dictated by the authority figures in my life. Within those constraints, my hair was the only signifier I could control. Its movement and length made me feel sexual and provocative. I loved how it hid secrets, like the tiny forbidden earrings I wore each day, flouting the possibility of detention.

Today my haircut will be a co-construction by my Japanese hairstylist and myself. We go back to the beginning, 2014, to find something to move us forward. After today my hair is short, like it was then. When it's tucked behind my ears, I channel Twiggy. I have hidden undercuts, which feel like having a secret and allow me to surprise when I style my hair upward or slicked back. It's close to my skull in some places and long in others, allowing me to play with all my extremes and all my ambivalence.

Jun and I take photos. The haircut is the same but different from the one I had before. My hair is whiter. In the photos I take now, me in my new short haircut fills only half of the frame. Calvin fills the other half. His black hair, gray at the temples, goes down almost to his waist. As we stand together, me with my short hair and his so long, I imagine my mother's smile. My hair, like myself, never remains the same. It is with me as I reimagine a new story. It is an "our" story as Calvin and I embark on our new adventure, our respective hairstyles an invitation for others to think differently.

My grandson's head is very round. He is plump and juicy, like a peach. His skin is the whitest of white. His eyes are blue like mine. His smile, which I can elicit whenever we look at each other, cracks his face open like a ripe fruit, filling the room with the perfume of delight. His delicious sweetness takes away all the bitterness of the world right now. He teaches me patience as I learn the meaning of every sound, each gesture, the pitch of a cry. When his little body moves into mine, I too become soothed and suffused with peace as he does.

If I weren't writing a book, facing deadlines, I'd enjoy and taste every fruit in this garden and just let that be how I live each day. Life intrudes as it always does. I pull a muscle from constantly leaning over to change a diaper. Yet I will never have these days again. He is at the beginning of his life, and I am approaching the beginning of the end of mine. Not soon, mind you, but as you know, I'm pragmatic. When his sister was born, eight years before, I did not feel old, as I do now. I state this without judgment or fear, knowing this realization makes each day more meaningful, more important. This is probably the last time I'll care for a baby containing my DNA. I can't foresee any more in my life except for the new, tantalizingly possible thought that I might be here in twenty or thirty years, in which case there could be a great-grandchild. It is 6:00. My delectable fruit is about to arrive. My arms twitch in anticipation. I can't wait to nuzzle my nose in his neck.

We are all in Austin, gathered for the wedding of my niece. It is the first big family event since the death of my mother. The bride and groom have asked me to officiate because I am the family member who most shares the bride and groom's activist leanings. I've always been very close to my niece because of this. My daughter and granddaughter are part of the wedding party. My siblings are here. The weather is beautiful, yet the absence of my mother hangs in the air. I wear a bright blue three-tiered dress with orange pumps and give a wedding speech that makes people laugh, notes all the grandparents that have passed, evidences my understanding of my niece and the relationship she has with her new partner, includes references to the life they share on Instagram and their passion for their dog, and encourages them to indulge in the sloppiest of kisses. It surprises many in the audience that someone my age would speak so easily, in a way that flies in the face of tradition.

I sit at the head of the "family" table and realize I am probably the oldest person in the room. Nieces and nephews ask if I need a drink or something to eat. My daughter knows better and steps aside to let me prepare a dish for my granddaughter from the Tex-Mex buffet. Since the death of my mother, I am now the matriarch of my family. If history repeats, during holidays and special occasions I will sit the entire time in a comfortable chair. People will bring me plates of food. Someone will drive me home early, while others stay behind to play games and laugh until their stomachs hurt. No longer am I expected to help clean up, do the dishes, or prepare the meal. They will let me fold laundry, but that's about it. Presents will include books, comfortable sweatshirts, and countless pairs of slippers and scarves.

The DJ starts the music, the bride and groom start the dance, and the floor fills up. My granddaughter has been waiting for this moment and gravitates toward the bride, her beloved godmother. One by one, every generation is on the dance floor. It's a mix of varying dance moves: disco fingers, moonwalk, electric slide, break-dancing courtesy of my brother-in-law, vogueing (thank you, Madonna), hip-hop, and TikTok dance trends. I'm pretty good at them all, although I am now just learning the TikTok ones. Time for me to get up there and show them how it's really done. Before too long, everyone on the dance floor is doing the Bump.

When restoring my new/old house, I spend the most time designing my kitchen and outdoor dining room. While I will let the next generation take over some of the holiday gatherings, I am not willing to concede them all, and I will still help to prepare the meal, wash the dishes, and stay around for the games. As I design it, I envision my kitchen filled with many hands making the food, some smooth and supple, others more delicate, with translucent skin. Calvin's supportive presence is an ingredient in everything I do, every meal I make. When there is a photo taken of me now, he is in it too. There are stories shared; of new experiences and remembrances of some from the past. Love will spill into the dining room and out into the yard.

My granddaughter will gather the herbs she planted to season the main course; my nephew will bartend and supply the craft beer he makes. I will bring my daughter a plate of food because she is tired from working full-time, breastfeeding, and having a baby who does not always sleep through the night. My niece will tell me about the new project she is working on; I will ask for her feedback on mine. My goddaughter will tell me about what it's like to be a nurse, and I will share stories of being a social worker. My sister will bring a side dish, one brother the wine, and someone else will contribute dessert. I will set a spectacular table using my mother's china so we may have her in the room. Rather than sit, I will stand at the center of the room, command it, and make a toast to the four generations that fill it. I will probably laugh the loudest and be the most competitive during the games that follow. I will not be leaving or going to bed anytime soon.

Epilogue

As I turn seventy, I imagine the clothes I will wear that help me tell the story of the decade I am about to enter, that add chapters to the ongoing memoir of my life that hangs on a rack upstairs. Somehow I sense that what I get dressed in will be new/old, like my house, my garden, the persona of Accidental Icon. That how I decide to dress will change over time, as I will. The next decade stretches before me like a new blank notebook, waiting to be filled with classes to be taken, essays to be written, mistakes to be made, and serendipitous occurrences. There will be losses and gains, good times and bad. I will probably lose my way and find it again. I feel that little shiver of excitement that comes with asking myself, "What now?"

My new location upstate influences my clothing choice. It's a much slower rhythm here than in the city, more time spent in nature, and though my day is still full, it's less frenzied, a smoother flow. Right now, since I intend to live a long time, how I spend my money factors into decisions about what to wear. Seeing my grandchildren makes me always aware of how my decisions impact the earth. I can't forget the changing shape and parameters of my body as well. So part of getting dressed for me today needs to include a vision of where I am being old, how I am being old, how I want to be old.

Many women choose what to wear based on the lifestyle they embrace during any era of their life. If you're like me, you'll find garments from each of these times tucked away in the back of your closet. They are waiting to be found again and turned into something new. They contain remembrances of all the roles, the big events, stories told over the course of a life. When I worked in a law firm and would often be called to court to testify, being credible meant looking neat, well-groomed, and professional, with a tailored suit and minimal accessories and makeup. Clothes that could move as I ran after an active toddler or plopped down on the floor to play were what I often wore as a young mom. In my forties I took to wearing overalls, Converse high-tops, silk-screened velvet tops, and Kangol caps. When I was a doctoral student and professor, black-and-white clothes by Japanese designers reflected my intellectual strivings. Looking back, I realize each era had a kind of uniform shaped by context and suggesting who I was or aspired to be.

Yet while wearing each of these particular "uniforms," I always found a way to make it mine and to add a bit of flair that challenged a rule but stayed within the lines. Wearing cowboy boots under the long pants of a suit as I walked into a courtroom. Overalls when I was forty. My style has always been a back-and-forth between others trying to define me through the demands of the context I find myself in and staking my claim about who I am and who I see myself becoming in that place. Society and systems will always try to write your narrative for you. As Accidental Icon, I found the line between costume and fashion, experimental yet elegant, rebellious yet dignified, being youthful without trying to look young. I suppose this back-and-forth is how I came to be known for having a unique sense of style. It's how I told a different story about how to be old.

Now, because of the pandemic, critical reflections, the death of my mother, changes in my body, and turning seventy, I experiment with finding a uniform again. With the move outside the city, I have fewer events, meetings, and formal engagements. As I have given up "influencing," I no longer feel a demand to get dressed to produce content because I have to do an Instagram post. I experiment with living on what I already have and being creative in how we are recycling and upcycling the restoration and renovation of our home. Living with less means I engage even more with everyday creativity, experiences, and people. My life is now centered on my partner, my home, my wild and overgrown garden, my daughter and grandchildren, writing, becoming involved in my community, and being purposeful and diligent about the things I need to do so I can continue to be old in a healthy and satisfied way.

Recently I have been wearing gardening clogs with my oldest, most faded pair of denim jeans and a silk pajama top.

My explorations into ecoliteracy reassure me that I am not a slob because I do not wash my jeans, even though I wear them every day. My research has revealed that washing jeans less frequently is beneficial for the planet. The pajama top is a washed palette of pastels that suggest flowers blooming in the gentle spring light. Pairing this with my jeans makes me feel seductive, free of constraint, androgynous, and, yes, elegant.

With all the heaviness in the world around me, the soft lightness of the silk hanging from my shoulders is all the load I feel like carrying right now. The shirt doesn't place a demand; it asks no questions that need urgent answers, no immediate return text expected, and for that I am grateful. These clothes allow me to indulge the aimless wandering and reimagining about how to find wonder in the everyday. The soft pastel flowers blur and remind me of my love of watercolors. Their fragility and whispered renderings are a gentle nudge to slow down, rather than a hard push. To slow down so you may stop, think, and contemplate. Pay attention, observe. My shirt elegantly dismisses that unrelenting push that says keep striving, be productive. Because this shirt is one half of a pair of pajamas, it is telling me I must rest and take time to recover when I need to. To embrace loss, and when I am ready, find something that brings me pleasure to fill in the space.

There is something about the weight and texture of my denim jeans that is grounding. They contain layers of experiences. They gain their unique character through being worn and used, as do we. Jeans began as something we wear when we need to work outside. The weaving process, the washes, the details of a particular brand, make every pair of denim jeans unique. Over time, denim remains one of the most functional and durable fabrics. Its color, indigo, is one of the oldest dyes to be used on textiles. Denim always appears in some form in fashion shows and has developed into many forms. We find jeans in most people's closets. They transcend race, class, age, and gender. They increase in value over time.

Jeans for me, as a teenager in the 1970s, were a symbol of rebellion and nonconformity, particularly compared to most girls in my high school, who preferred the more preppie look during our uniform off-hours. Slung low on my hips with wide bell-like flares, they made me feel sexy and cool. Perhaps therefore I do not now, or ever, favor the high-waisted or skinny variety. Oversize is a must, so there is room to grow. While I may no longer feel like the cocky badass I was as a teenager or as Accidental Icon in my sixties, I feel strong and in control, and I remain, as always, defiant of what society tells me I should do as I begin my seventies.

My current favorite denim jeans are recycled, baggy wide-leg with ripped knees and jagged tears, waiting to be mended. I have seam-ripped many pairs I own that no longer fit. The years of the decade fall away into pieces that are the parts of the "garments" I've worn as a professor, a social worker, an influencer, writer, mother, grandmother, granddaughter, daughter, partner, sister, friend, and colleague. I see what parts of each "garment" remain true and right and what parts no longer fit or meet my needs. The parts of them that are now contained in a large basket will ultimately become something else. I've become quite an expert at using a seam ripper. When you become proficient with a seam ripper, mistakes become opportunities to redo, reinvent, and upcycle. When garments burst at the seams, rip, or fall apart, they present a creative challenge. While repairing flaws is one benefit of upcycling clothes, upcycling goes beyond repairing an item. Upcycling is a hopeful process because when you reinvent something old and make it something new and more valuable, you are expanding the life it has already lived.

In the early mornings, I write. In the afternoons, I pick up a needle and search through my box of brightly colored embroidery thread. I transfer old photos of Accidental Icon, objects that engaged her, clothes she wore, and places she traveled to on cotton squares. I embroider bright red lips; fill in sunglasses with tiny black stitches. Sometimes I embroider big earrings and embellish them with beads. I transfer photos I've taken of my garden, scenes from the Hudson Valley towns we visit, pumpkins, quilts, and a beating heart. I embroider words and phrases from the many books I have time to read now that make me catch my breath. These worked-upon patches peek through the curtain of the remaining threads of the tears. These patches repair and renew my old denim jeans. They make them something new and never seen before. They write a new chapter in the story they already tell.

I will include my patches on anything else I might become inspired to make with my pieces of old denim jeans; a coat perhaps, or a long apron. I access old memories in the service of something new. Fresh memories accessed in the service of something old.

When I engage with the stories my old denim jeans tell, I find the secrets I look for that tell me how to be old. My experiments with them now will reveal even more. This, I realize, is why I wear them all the time. My denim jeans and I are layered with meaning, memories; past, current, and potential selves. We increase in value as we grow older. My denim jeans and I are so much more than just our age. We use our memories and histories to propel and energize the dynamic process of growing old. How we think about the changes that occur as we age determines how we respond to them. The most interesting lessons in the years I just experienced and remembered about how to be old show the reality that being old is not a constant, nor does it hold steady. We each, depending on who we may be and our varying degrees of privilege, experience it differently. Learning how to be old does not have a specific age because getting older, which we do from the moment we are born, is a fluctuating process of responding, adapting, and negotiating as your body, relationships, opportunities, and challenges change. When we think about being old, we often cannot remember that life is always unpredictable. We forget that identities, including being old, remain fluid, not set in stone. Being old is the same but different from other times in a life. Today

Dior reached out to me to do a post. They are debuting a new jewelry collection and want to feature me as a "writer," not an "influencer." I agree to do it, and as I do, I accept this new identity. I make a choice.

Acceptance for me today means I am always on intimate terms with younger versions of myself. I am on intimate terms with what is currently my older self. I am on intimate terms with my potential future older selves. I imagine them; I fear them; I design for them; I mourn them; I reminisce about them; I celebrate them; I expect them; I plan for them. I dress them. I live with them all. In this way, I defy chronology. I defy an imposed structure of age. I am a rebel and a refuser. I guess you could call me belligerent. I am my mother's daughter. Acceptance for me at twenty-five under these terms would have meant not just being intimate with my younger and current self but inviting my future older self to join the party. To dance with her the way I do when my younger nieces and nephews and now my granddaughter pull me up on the dance floor at family weddings. We become a knot of women from all generations, laughing and dancing as fast as we can.

Acknowledgments

I would like to thank my incredibly patient agent, Mollie Glick, for never giving up on the idea that I had a book in me. This book would never have been what it has become without the insight and inspiration so gracefully and respectfully imparted by my editor, Cassidy Sachs. I thank my partner Calvin, my daughter, my son-in-law, and my family, who support me in everything I ever want to do. My grandson and granddaughter motivate me to want to leave this world a better place for them every day, and bring me more joy than I ever could imagine. I have much gratitude for my writing friends Christine Platt and Latonya Yvette, who supplied pearls of writing wisdom, laughs, and love. Finally, I want to acknowledge all my followers who have supported me these past ten years, helped me believe I was a writer, and encouraged me to write a book. They continue to provide me with endless inspiration through their willingness to share their amazing stories of reinvention and resilience, as well as an unending stream of creative ideas about how to be old. Together we are rewriting the narrative of what it means to be an older woman today.

About the Author

Lyn Slater is a cultural influencer, model, writer, content creator, and former professor. She started *Accidental Icon* in September 2014 and has since garnered a loyal fan base of almost a million followers across platforms.